Managing and Leading for
Science Professionals

Managing and Leading for Science Professionals

(What I Wish I'd Known When Moving Up the Management Ladder)

Bertrand C. Liang, MD, PhD, MBA

AMSTERDAM • BOSTON • HEIDELBERG • LONDON
NEW YORK • OXFORD • PARIS • SAN DIEGO
SAN FRANCISCO • SINGAPORE • SYDNEY • TOKYO

Academic Press is an Imprint of Elsevier

Academic Press is an imprint of Elsevier
The Boulevard, Langford Lane, Kidlington, Oxford, OX5 1GB, UK
525 B Street, Suite 1900, San Diego, CA 92101-4495, USA

First edition 2014

British Library Cataloguing in Publication Data
A catalogue record for this book is available from the British Library

Library of Congress Cataloging-in-Publication Data
A catalog record for this book is available from the Library of Congress

ISBN–13: 978-0-12-416686-8

For information on all Academic Press publications
visit our website at books.elsevier.com

Working together
to grow libraries in
developing countries

ELSEVIER   Book Aid International

www.elsevier.com • www.bookaid.org

To my amazing family, whose exploits
are as much motivational as
they are truly remarkable.

A Leadership Prayer

Give me the vision to see what is needed;
The opportunities to set and meet the right goals;
Motivate and encourage,
While guiding and directing;
And hear what is being said.
Help me recognize and shun mediocrity;
To keep to the mission at hand;
To embrace change and not hold to tradition;
And remember that to take no risk
Is the biggest risk of them all.

Contents

15. A Final Note   **149**

Companion Website for this Book:
http://booksite.elsevier.com\9780124166868

"Unprovided with original learning, uninformed in the habits of thinking, unskilled in the arts of composition, I resolved to write a book".

-Edward Gibbon

There are many management books lining the shelves of bookstores and libraries encompassing the theories and hypotheses regarding those skills required to be effective and productive. Excellent texts exist around motivation, communication, change management *etc.*, which reflect the importance of these areas in the vast diversity of organizations today. And this is not limited merely to Fortune 100 firms, small-cap commercial organizations, or private companies; we see that universities, trade associations, and governments as well as non-governmental organizations now have programs encompassing management and leadership. Training programs in these latter types of organizations suggest the realization that lessons from the business (and military) world may indeed be transferred to the development of strategy and execution of tactics in non-commercial settings. However, the refinements of management theory, originating in the different management schools and universities, provide an at times bewildering array of choices upon which managers and manager-to-be s (or want-to-be s) may choose in order to begin or continue their specific journey toward value creation in a group or group setting. The key is to make the choice, and follow through with the understanding that many concepts may be within a rubric where a new perspective is required.

Within this context is the idea that technical personnel are the same, but different. It is my humble observation – having been on both the scientific and commercial ladder – that the science/engineering ecosystem inherently emphasizes different things, putting such professionals at a distinct disadvantage compared to the commercial part of the organization. This is not purposeful, but a result of the very nature of the R&D process and the way we reward technical staff; it tends to be, from training onward, an individual or small group affair, focused on distinct "right" and "wrong" answers. We center on individual efforts, from graduate school to post-doc days (to get our names in prominent positions on publications), or from working on prototypes to projects where reductionist efforts allow components to be created only to be reconstructed later on. Individual effort, while not exclusive, is emphasized; we need to be able to show our scientific or engineering competence by getting the data...and the right answer. This can be contrasted by efforts in the commercial part of the organization, where a team orientation is almost always required in every project, and where results have distinct levels of risk and uncertainty. Training in business school encompasses by definition team efforts, whether analyzing cases to collaboration on projects; I cannot recall any assignment in which I was involved that did not have at least some cooperative aspect within it. Decisions on cases while requiring analysis and justification can often have diverse outcomes based on assumptions and interpretations made. The tacit understanding is that the team is the way to get things done, rather than *via* the individual *per se*; individual effort is expected, but the way to the promised land is through collective effort; consensus is about grey areas, where black and white areas are the exception. It is thus no surprise that this results in commercial staff adapting to organizational structures more easily than the technical, and as a general observation, start as better managers than those on the technical side.

I certainly know that this was reflected in the way I learned about and rose through different technically oriented organizations. What I realized was that management – dealing with people and the challenges inherent in those interactions – was fundamentally missing in our training as scientists, whether as a student, post-doc, R&D manager, or vice president, wherein this was inculcated on the commercial side. And leadership, *i.e.* being able to motivate, articulate a vision, and requisite goals for the organization, while present, was rarely central. Impractical as it might be, it would have been probably better to rise initially on the commercial side of the organization, rather than the R&D side, since those people skills were so important to develop and clearly applicable throughout the firm.

Hence, this book was born, not necessarily to preach about teams or how technical staff are different, or even "how to be" a better manager (although certainly, it is hoped this is the result). Instead, this is much more a pragmatic approach of *what I wished I'd known* when I was rising through the ranks, especially on the R&D side of the organization and transitioning to the commercial/ corporate one. As noted, there are great books that describe well how "geeks" are different, or strategies to approach scientists. However, this book aims to *address the manager and leader* within the technical side of the organization, who might be managing people for the first time, or all of a sudden have been put in a position to manage many people (some of whom may not even be within R&D!). By understanding how our scientific training can either help, or hurt, our performance *via* our biases, we can know better how to channel our efforts toward making our organizations the best they can be, by facilitation, encouragement, hearing, and motivating (as well as being technically competent). Our organizations have placed confidence in us with recognition and responsibilities; we owe our firms, as a result, no less than that.

I want to thank my supportive family, without whom either the inspiration or motivation would have existed to push this project to completion. Moreover, like any such project, this one represents much generosity of time from very busy people who were gracious enough to speak with me. Many colleagues and acquaintances provided their feedback and thoughts, which have been greatly appreciated and provided more color and clarity than I could have come up with alone. For fruitful discussions and reviews, I appreciate the input of Dan Bradbury (BioBrit), Michael Hough (Advance Medical), Oscar Velastegui (Pfizer), Phil Perera (Dart Neuroscience), Kevin McElgunn (Dow), Xavier Frapaise (EULexer), Patrick Lucy (Pfenex), Ana Zambelli (TransOcean), Robin Robinson (BARDA), and Court Chilton (SloanMIT); for the introduction of the Myers-Briggs Type Indicator, I thank Margi Mainquist (Mainquist Consulting); and finally, a special thanks to Shinya Yano, who agreed to write the foreword from many miles and time zones away. A most sincere thanks to my editor, Dr. Scott Bentley, and the staff at Elsevier, for their professionalism and expertise throughout this process. I finally thank those mentors, peers, mentees, and reports who have taught me both about leadership and management (of people and myself), often without even knowing they were doing so (including those represented in this book). You remain an inspiration, and remind me that I can always do better.

The nature of the challenges for technical executives moving into management ranks often reflect both a language and cultural gap, as well as a transformation from a focused view to that of a "bird's eye" view of the corporation. We often see this with the true variety of people that one encounters when beginning a managerial career, where often communication can be challenging, even when we think we are using the same language, based on the personalities of those involved whether they are in the basic or applied science departments, marketing or even business development. As scientists, we must truly see outside ourselves and be very careful in how we view situations remote to the scientific realm, understanding that we must be more general (but still accurate) in both explanation and interpretation. What is clear is that the approach we use if we have started within the scientific part of the firm and are now taking a managerial role is one not only of translation (of science to either business or layman terms) but also to insure understanding by colleagues with different areas of expertise. This is a distinctive psychology than that used when discussing scientific experiments with laboratory personnel, where understanding is assumed, and it is one that we as scientists must often learn as we move to being a company manager.

As well, there are other skills that new managers need to be aware of within their new positions. These vary from how to interact with new reports to interfacing and having a customer oriented view; from being able to make decisions when all of the information is not present, to being able to view the company widely, understanding different perspectives. These are not easy transitions, and in particular, are not those we have typically been taught in university or even in the corporate laboratory setting. Only by being able to appreciate, understand, and adapt to these new requirements can we best realize the science into concrete ways to create business value.

Bert's book is a welcome and unique offering into this area, helping new scientific managers both become better and evolve through some of the most difficult areas they may encounter. Scientific managers who either stay within or move away from scientific disciplines must appreciate and acquire new skills quickly and be able to work with their team members, playing not only the role of translator, but of facilitator, consensus builder, and teacher, most often in different but sometimes in the same situation. This book is well designed specifically to help these aspiring leaders in the company, and provides a firm basis for those who have decided to enter into the management track. It will help those who would be leaders, managers and in the case of the extraordinary and lucky (sometimes unlucky) people, CEOs, begin their fascinating challenges from the bench to the corporate office.

The changes in the business climate occur quickly, and our responses need to be as fast in order to remain competitive. Speed is important since company personnel from all parts of the organization and especially those in corporate to board of director roles have limited time to make decisions. Bert's book represents an excellent way for a new manager and leader from the scientific part of the company to learn and anticipate those challenges before him or her, and not only survive the transformation, but thrive within it.

Shinya Yano, PhD
Former CEO
Astellas Venture Management
Head of Scientific Intelligence, Product and Portfolio Strategy
Astellas Pharma Inc.
Tokyo, Japan

The Road to Success is the Road to Failure

"At the heart of science is an essential balance between two seemingly contradictory attitudes – an openness to new ideas, no matter how bizarre or counterintuitive they may be, and the most ruthless skeptical scrutiny of all ideas, old and new. This is how deep truths are winnowed from deep nonsense".

-Carl Sagan

"We must discard the idea that past routine, past ways of doing things, are probably the best ways. On the contrary, we must assume that there is probably a better way to do almost everything. We must stop assuming that a thing that has never been done before probably cannot be done at all".

-Donald M. Nelson

"We don't see many fat men walking on stilts".

-Bud Miller

Cliff, the Molecular Biology Superstar

You could always depend on Cliff to come up with a killer experiment, or get the data from a particularly difficult technique or procedure. He was the "go to" guy when the team needed a creative solution or approach to tackle a challenging molecular biology problem to move the program forward. Relatively young, he was promoted to being a group leader, with a team of two PhD level scientists and one technician, focused on cloning a particular gene that had proved very challenging. Several months after being promoted, Cliff appeared burned out. Walking into his lab, there was little conversation, with the two PhD scientists (if they were there at all) whispering to one another at their desks, which abutted their respective lab benches. Cliff and his technician were often seen at the technician's bench, involved in an experiment, or in his office, huddled over data. Previously known as someone who occasionally would organize informal talks, he no longer participated in even departmental seminars, and was seen to be in the lab late at night. At the end of his first year, he announced that he had indeed cloned the gene of which the project was focused, and had already done some initial characterization of the gene product. To his boss, he confided that the scientists in his lab had contributed little, and that their lack of data made it impossible to characterize whether their scientific abilities were any good. While Cliff did note that the technician in the lab had performed well under his supervision, on a feedback survey, both the technician and the scientists rated him a 1 out of 5 on all areas with the exception of knowledge base, where he was ranked 5 out of 5. At the end of year review, Cliff was surprised at his negative evaluation, and noted that, in fact, the gene upon which the project was focused had been cloned. What was the problem?

SHOULDN'T SUCCESS BE BASED ON CREATING DATA?

We as scientists and/or engineers are task oriented. Usually, there is a problem to be solved, and a program that requires advancement, where thoughtful diligence and experimentation is key in order to at least arrive at an approach, if not a solution, to a given effort. We probably all recall times and episodes when either as a graduate student, early stage engineer, intern, or resident, we were called upon to be able to create, produce, or identify data necessary to facilitate progress, and were either rewarded when we were able to get over the finish line with such programs, or provided with negative reinforcement if unable to do so. Our direct efforts clearly were part of our success, and the ability to produce actionable information was clearly valued. Hence, by the very nature of the scientific endeavor, the positive reinforcement is upon our personal successes on task achievement, *i.e.* getting to the goal or objective that was put before us, as a prototype, experiment, or even cloning of a gene.

This ability to get the job done is reinforced as we move into specific roles within different organizations. Today, almost all of us have worked on a team, and our contributions (hopefully!) add synergistically (in the positive sense of the word) to the project at hand. As more junior members of the team, however, we still have as a goal to perform at a high level individually, in our respective functional areas.

The challenge we face, as did Cliff, was that the abilities that were so prevalent toward his success as a scientist were the same as all of us have experienced as either individual contributors or junior members of any team. Being the "go to" guy is certainly perceived to be a great thing – it implies technical competence, high levels of diligence, and/or creativity. We promote individuals because of these abilities and as a result of these implications. But the issue inherent in our system of rewards is that as valuable as this is, it causes issues when used at a higher level. We are so accustomed to being successful in our efforts that having to trust others to do what we know we can do ourselves is an

TABLE 1.1 Four Quick Questions Related to Team/Group Participation

Am I spending most of my time advising, assisting, and assessing in the project?
Is my motivation toward completion of the project, or credit for the project?
Have I articulated the project goals to the team and have responsibilities been assigned?
Have I set up the project as a "coordination vehicle", around which we all can rally?

anathema; why rely on anyone else when we have been able to be successful ourselves? And if we don't rely on others who report to us, can't we control the process more easily and efficiently? Obviously, there are many issues associated with these scenarios. Amongst others, we don't spend time mentoring our reports so that they can develop and achieve their own goals; we propagate a sense of self-reliance (*i.e.* self-worth) at the expense of the group; we *demotivate with success*, since it's a factor of an individual and not the team effort; and we ourselves don't develop as managers, knowing how to ensure participation in a project, and grow by being able to advise, assist, and assess others.

Hence, while our systems on the technical side of the organization reward achievement, they oftentimes create situations where managers will fail just by using the strategies that allowed them to succeed in the first place. New managers need to recognize these issues and create opportunities for reports and themselves to develop. This takes time, patience, and a different view of the world than when strictly "on the shop floor", as the latter is not sustainable for either the group leader or reports. Our perspective needs to evolve both to keep our focus and integrate the efforts of others. So while success is initially reliant upon creating data, it is maintained by developing other skills related to a collective effort. Table 1.1 shows some questions to be asked to understand one's own motivations toward a given project or program.

Principal Investigator as Principal Manager: The EMBO Program

Since 2004, the European Molecular Biology Organization (EMBO) has made available management courses targeted at junior investigators in the biomedical sciences. Initially for either those who had been chosen for the Young Investigator Program, or the European Molecular Biology Laboratory group leaders, the program was extended to include other post-doctoral fellows as well. The course has expanded to a five-day format from two days, covering a myriad of different topics such as time and project management, lab leadership, and conflict management; it has subsequently increased in scope to involve people management, including role playing and dealing with subordinates, such as students and other trainees. EMBO leadership noted that management training was neglected in most if not all

Continued

Principal Investigator as Principal Manager: The EMBO Program—cont'd

training programs, and the level of subsequent opportunities was extremely limited. While all participants were focused on or within an academic environment, the skills around communication, empowerment, and delegation were found to be very important in order to ensure beneficial relationships, even in times of interpersonal conflict. The course has been very popular at all levels, and has so far been fully registered each time it is offered. Using management skills within academic environments has been found to be valuable, and will hopefully portend to investigators who will be able to motivate and facilitate their laboratory members to higher levels of productivity.

Forde, A. *Training Scientists as Managers. Science Career Magazine: The Job Market,* July 15, 2005.

THE DECEPTION OF PERCEPTION

At least initially, we as technical personnel often look to be expert in our own fields. Again, this is part of the need to be perceived as a resource as well as a contributor; being knowledgeable about one's field is part and parcel of this need. This makes sense as it is clearly part of being a scientist or engineer; you are valued for your analytical abilities, your domain knowledge, and sophisticated understanding of R&D. Cliff was clearly valued for his abilities as a problem solver and his knowledge base; this was one of the areas by which even as a group leader, noted by his direct reports, he did quite well.

In science and engineering, this is highly reinforced. To some, it is a point of pride to be able to bring to the table the latest journal article from *IEEE Transactions*, quote from a *New England Journal of Medicine* article on a point needed for the design of a clinical trial, or recall a patent that is directly applicable to the second generation prototype at hand. As a marketing colleague once quipped, "Your jobs are to be the smartest guys in the room". Interestingly, this is how we gain respect amongst our peers, and how we assess others within the organization. The need to be an expert is engrained in our scientific training and reward system, and creates the perception that this is a key relevant factor in all of our interactions. It is why oftentimes we advance someone's career, and provide him or her additional responsibility, *viz.* due to their perceived intelligence and knowledge in a particular area. As noted with Cliff, he was promoted despite his relatively young age, precisely because he was seen as a relied upon intelligent performer.

While functional area expertise is by far the most common reason for advancement, it is also the reason why many technical managers fail. The perceived need to maintain the highest level of technical competence, especially at significant levels in the organization, is both difficult and fraught with peril. Many management texts note the need to communicate and motivate as part of leadership and management (discussed in Chapter 2); however, for technical executives, adding these skills along with having to master a new mindset around relying on others and expecting to be able to, for example, write code or get a western blot to be successful, is at best difficult, and nary impossible without neglecting other aspects of inherent responsibilities. As a manager, one has to realize that for the best interests of the group, and for the organization, those "soft" management texts have a reason for articulating the need for communication and motivation; that is the key job as one moves up the ladder; it is a realization that needs to be identified and actively communicated to managers on the technical side of the organization. While this is not to suggest that losing all technical expertise is desired or appropriate (it's not!), the perspective needs to change, emphasizing the facilitation of the groups' work, rather than being able to answer every question regarding details in a scientific area. Being able to help locate an answer or solution to a problem is still certainly a skill to be embraced, but expecting to maintain the level of a detailed technical expert is both unrealistic, and frankly undesirable. The opportunity cost of doing so is simply too high, and groups (and organizations) can suffer as a result (see Figure 1.1). A very perceptive colleague once held a meeting with his group to announce he would be promoted into a role that would encompass several of the R&D areas; he wore black, and had a cake with a tombstone that had his area of specialty named. He clearly understood that his ability to engage on the detailed workings of his technical areas was not going to be possible any longer, but that he would be expected to be broader in scope and emphasize a different skill set. This was something that perhaps would have been better for Cliff's supervisor to proactively identify for him, rather than letting him find out for himself after his (demotivating) "success".

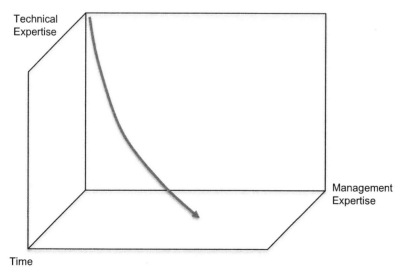

FIGURE 1.1   Decline in technical expertise with increased management expertise over time.

PERFECT IS THE ENEMY OF GOOD ENOUGH

In my past, I can recall a time when I delayed the submission of a publication because one of the data gels had a distinct streak across it, which while not obscuring the band (which represented the data) still did not look particularly attractive; hence, I had to repeat an experiment to create a better looking image (these were the days before Photoshop). I recall submitting the paper after about a month delay, only to see that, several months later, I had been "scooped" by another lab whose data was similar to (but less pretty) than mine. While disappointed, this was the beginning of my understanding that good can be good enough, and that perfection can be ephemeral. Like anyone else in the organization, we as scientists or engineers in general have a pride of ownership of our work; this is reflected in the materials we show in presentations and the data we present in print or other forms. It is important that we depict our data as solid and high quality to maintain our credibility within our areas. Our personae are displayed in the data, products, prototypes, or even beta versions of our efforts.

That being said, it is clear that perfection may not, cannot, or should not be achieved in the development of programs. There are often other reasons why moving forward is more important than being perfect; timelines, costs of reiteration, an unachievable target can all be reason enough to have to "settle" for a product that meets only the minimal target product profile, as much as the desire to have something better as desired by marketing or internally within R&D is articulated. As managers, the need to be able to qualify what meets the organizational need is often against the urge of scientific perfection. Our training tends to demand of us perfection, but it is clear that this should be tempered with other needs, which might require the modification of our perspectives. Conversely, however, perfection on a technical scale may not be commercially viable; building a prototype that addresses an issue for a customer that is so resource intense to be economically prohibitive might solve a problem but not create a solution. As managers, we need to be cognizant of the requirements of the organization, fully understanding that while R&D is expected to be creative and sophisticated, we must work within a framework relevant to an entire organization, including the strategy, objectives, and goals thereof. While striving for perfection is an ongoing goal, understanding the practicalities of the need to press forward and create value should temper our efforts. Fundamental communication with other parts of the organization (see Chapter 9) can be extraordinarily helpful in this regard.

BEING COMPLETE DOESN'T MEAN BEING COMPLICATED

It has been noted that there has been more information created in the past 30 years than in the previous 5000. Moore's Law (as modified by House) notes that the increase in doubling in chip performance (a combination of more transistors and being faster) occurs about *every 18 months*. This growth requires a level of sophistication, particularly in those who generate, interpret, evaluate, and disseminate such information. Those of us who work in the technical part of the organization are very much integrated into this *milieu*; our jobs reflect this essence. The nature of the endeavor often, then, requires us to modify and innovate in order to utilize these advances. Interestingly, as part of the fact noted earlier, accompanying all that information generation over the past three decades, the number of new *words* has increased (as have additional definitions for old words, *e.g.* mouse, brick, bug, google to name a few) by a logfold at least, from when dictionaries required a word to be cited once a year for five years running to be included in a new edition. Certainly, this reflects the needs of novel technologies and processes to be described and articulated precisely, particularly with innovations not existing previously. While other fields of endeavor from management to marketing have these same issues, it is arguably not to the same degree as that within the technical arena (although vocabulary certainly is different between these areas as well).

The expansion of our technological sophistication is shown in our publications and other communication rubrics. These have become quite complex elaborations on information being generated, requiring a knowledge base that is becoming more specialized on a daily basis. A senior manager (since retired) who was leading an R&D area recently noted to me that she now understands better the articles from the management journals received more than the scientific ones in her area of technical expertise; obviously, this reflects both an increasing sophistication of her management skills, but also suggests the complexity of the scientific data being generated is certainly increasing (exponentially).

It is thus one of the largest challenges for technical personnel to "de-complicate", *viz.* simplify concepts and data, which we will return to several times within this book. Being complete, with all the inherent levels of sophistication needed, is part of the scientific endeavor. However, as one moves up the managerial ranks, it is clear that there is a dichotomy between efficient transfer of information and the time required for full measure of articulating that information. While we may know the very depths of the details surrounding the buildout of the second or third generation mock-up, or the magnesium concentrations (and effects) on a polymerase chain reaction experiment, it is imperative that we recall the quip noted from my former senior management colleague regarding the decreasing understanding of the scientific articles due to their inherent complexity. It is that our audience will typically be more senior, with the requisite concentrations on other facets of the R&D work – either being more general in management and/or scientific approach. Our ability to simplify concepts and information – despite our growing up in an environment where the details really do matter – is a hugely valued skill, for efficiency, clarity to those not skilled in the area, and to potential external audiences. This is part of the communication abilities noted in management books across many facets of an organization, but one that is not particularly emphasized from an R&D point of view. This is either a skill that a technical executive must add to his or her armamentarium, or one that has to be pulled back into the fold from when as a graduate student having to teach fledgling undergraduate students. In this case, while communication should have the components many leadership and management texts profess (*e.g.* clarity, planning, relation to objectives, *etc.*) the technical manager must simplify for the audience at hand; it is much easier to add detail after having a concept understood, than to do the reverse.

Michael was a highly respected basic researcher in the area of hematology. He had had a significant academic career, becoming a professor of medicine, and was looking to branch out to commercialize some of his findings in a new company he had started. While he had an "upper Midwest charm", naming his company after his hometown in the Midwest, his dedication to academic accuracy was, to say the least, daunting. His initial presentation to potential investors for his company was over 60 slides long, with detailed maps of metabolic pathways that were more complete than textbooks; he spoke with authority (in a professorial manner) around the basic science of the disease entities to be addressed, and concluded his presentation with the amount of money he was looking to raise. Despite Michael's patience with questions, he was unable to raise any investment for his company, and after about 6 months, "simplified" his presentation to 35 slides. When one firm did ask him to return for a second presentation, Michael returned to the 60 slide tome despite receiving advice that the result might be similar to what had occurred previously. Feedback by investors was uniform regarding the complexity of his presentations, and lack of commercial focus; while Michael seemed to understand this, he always returned to notions about portraying the "completeness" of background and data when discussing his presentation. He was not asked back to any other investment firm, and several years later, was angered to see that another group had obtained funding and done the clinical experiments in an academic setting that Michael had proposed during his fundraising efforts for his company. While the results were not exactly what Michael had predicted would occur, they were reasonably close, and this group did patent both the data from the experiment and further pursued the work in a corporate setting.

Michael clearly had issues with simplification, and felt the need to explain his scientific perspective in a detailed, complete fashion. Unfortunately, this completeness resulted in a complexity only the field cognoscenti could relate to and understand. The results and consequences were not unexpected, and despite Michael's chagrin, should have been anticipated as well. We as technical executives need to understand both the impact of jargon and miscommunication; a key responsibility we have is to be able to explain our data to the rest of the organization. Only with that ability will we serve the needs of our colleagues, and effect better decisions that are truly based on data.

"Fools ignore complexity. Pragmatists suffer it. Some can avoid it. Geniuses remove it".

-Alan Perlis

REFERENCES

Griffin, D., 2000. Complexity and Management: Fad or radical challenge to systems thinking? Complexity and Emergence in Organizations. Routledge, New York.

Morrel-Samuels, P., Francis, E., Shucard, S., 2009. Merged Datasets: An Analytical Tool For Evidence-based Management. California Management Review 52, 120–139.

Nel, W.P. (Ed.), 2006. Management for Engineers, Technologists and Scientists, second ed. Juta & Co., Cape Town.

Reay, T., Berta, W., Kohn, M., 2009. What's the Evidence on Evidence-Based Management? Academy of Management Perspectives 23, 5–18.

Management & Leadership

"You get the best out of others when you get the best out of yourself".

-Harvey S. Firestone

"I have three precious things which I hold fast and prize. The first is gentleness; the second is frugality; the third is humility, which keeps me from putting myself before others. Be gentle and you can be bold; be frugal and you can be liberal; avoid putting yourself before others and you can become a leader among men".

-Lao Tzu

"…good management is a bit like oxygen – it's invisible and you don't notice its presence until it's gone, and then you're sorry".

-Charles Stross

Ann, the detail-oriented manager

    Ann's careful and analytical approaches to her work were always valued by the group. She always checked and rechecked her work, and was ready at project meetings to be able to answer the most detailed questions about any technique or data set with which she had been involved. She had voluntarily taken courses on six sigma operations, and had worked to implement some of these principles in her own efforts. Because of the quality of her work, her attention to detail, and her interest in operational management, she was promoted to head a small group focusing on program operations, leading two others with similar backgrounds. From the beginning, there were significant issues. Ann would chair all meetings of which she and her direct reports were a part, no matter who set up the meeting. She would often interrupt others, both inside and outside the group, when she disagreed with a point, often prefacing her

Managing and Leading for Science Professionals. http://dx.doi.org/10.1016/B978-0-12-416686-8.00002-5
   11

remarks with, "Management believes…". Those reporting to her noted they were required to meet with Ann twice a day – once in the morning, for task "assignment", and once at the end of the day (convenient to her schedule), to determine what had been accomplished. She kept a spreadsheet, which outlined the "mistakes" each had made according to her estimate, and which she would report to her supervisor during their one-on-one meetings. Her supervisor, who had himself been recently promoted, noted her detail orientation positively but did not comment on her techniques of assessing her reports. Six weeks after her promotion, one of the program managers abruptly quit, leaving his laptop computer and a terse note on Ann's supervisor's desk, and a voicemail to the CEO. Ann was reassigned to another supervisor, who began working with her closely to clarify her role. But after the other program manager announced her intention of leaving within a week, Ann's responsibilities were removed and reassigned, and she was placed in a purely operational role, where she was required to inform her supervisor of all planned activities.

BEING THE BOSS

It has been said that one should not be limited by one's title, but by one's abilities. Nowhere does this apply better as a true meritocracy than in R&D, as the ability to measure one's productivity is defined (as noted) on results, at least in the context of data, publications, patents, *etc.* Taking on more responsibility *via* projects, helping others with their projects and programs (be it with techniques, guidance, identification of papers, and the like) is often *expected* in the laboratory, however. Indeed, the laboratory environment, particularly ones where there is an accumulation of post-doctoral fellows, graduate students, and undergraduates, articulates a given hierarchy that has as its pinnacle the lab director/professor/institute director. Indeed, this may be where we get our initial ideas of management and leadership, as fledgling students or post-docs. The lab director often holds the fate of all of the members of the lab in his figurative hand. He or she is the "boss" – writes and obtains grants/budgets, pays salaries, supervises (at least at some level), has say over what comes in and what goes out of the lab, *etc.* Indeed, in some labs, there is a reporting structure, where the lab director only interacts with the senior post-docs, and the latter with the junior ones, down the line to the undergraduate student doing a summer internship where he only talks to the graduate student(s). Nonetheless, for many in the sciences, this is a familiar situation, especially for those who worked in very large laboratories.

But as a paradigm, the student model is not a particularly good one vis-à-vis technical management, despite the fairly universal experiences in our scientific training. Often, the expectations of the laboratory director are unrealistically high, and there is actually negative reinforcement for a director to advance a student or fellow; if they are being trained in the lab, and taking time of the various personnel, keeping these people in the lab as long as possible is the best for return on investment. The *de minimus* "salaries" or stipends paid to these laboratory members is frequently below any minimum standard acceptable to governmental authorities, given the number of hours expected to be worked. As noted in Chapter 1, singular expression of success (despite any help received) is the important measure, in order to get one's name on a paper and/or finish a thesis of one sort or another. Not being self-motivated to push to "get out" can result in the status of "terminal post-doc" or "student for life", monikers also fairly universal to most training programs. While there are certainly many laboratory directors who truly mentor their students and fellows, there still exists the training-for-the-lab opportunity cost, and motivated (underpaid) labor, which does not necessarily portend to a model of leadership and management that provides the best example for the technical executive. As a newly minted PhD once noted, "It's like you're in prison; you have to find ways to get time off for good behavior (when discussing the lab director's direction of his project); that's how you graduate eventually".

Unfortunately, Ann's (extreme) idea on management (*micro*management) and control very much paralleled this model. Her newfound title created a sense of self-worth, which manifest as a need to manage through an authoritative lens, rather than by leadership or even a modicum of understanding of basic managerial principles (*e.g.,* tying into an overarching objective). Instead, she was the "boss", and her reports needed to become extensions of herself, rather than individuals attempting to accomplish a collective goal. While it is important to establish working relationships with one's reports in a way that provides clear understanding of reporting lines, given the allocation of responsibility, a title rarely (if ever) affords respect alone, particularly in R&D. Technical executives need to avoid situations both of Ann *and* her supervisor; the former because of the destructive results of her management style, and the latter because of the enablement and inferred acceptance of such a style. It clearly matters what approaches we use in our managerial, day-to-day interactions, and being either too restrictive or laissez-faire in our styles can be very counterproductive. Again, we are familiar with this type of management from earlier days in training; it should not, however, color our understanding of better styles that encompass solid business principles and practices that can result in more productive outcomes.

Being a Leader

Ann's case, and the ensuing discussion, begs the question of what is enough involvement and what is too much, or what is too little. However, despite the more extreme details of this case, it might be better to ask if leadership qualities could have been valuable here. Indeed, much has been written about leadership – definitions, qualities, ideals; still, it is ephemeral in some contexts when compared to the technical, data-driven aspects of the job(s) of the technical executive. And, as noted earlier, technical professionals often have a different standard by which they judge those with authority in an organization; there is, to an extent, a bar that has to be traversed based on technical or scientific competence.

There are excellent texts regarding different descriptions and qualities of leadership in the literature (see References). Fundamentally, many of the traits refer to the ability to articulate a vision, motivate, and communicate in a clear and concise manner (themes to which we will return multiple times throughout the book). Inherent in this is the clear formulation of an objective, whether it is the design of the next best-in-class product, to the creation of the next Fortune 100 company; it allows delineation of a strategy, which oftentimes requires a myriad of different components and areas of expertise. Indeed, this was a rationale to create and empower the (at the time) novel *matrix teams* at Boeing, by T.A. Wilson. The recognition of such goes beyond motivation, communication, and direction, to something deeper and more inherent with technical executives, which emphasizes that aforementioned need for competency, *viz.* expertise within a given discipline. It is clear, however, that this is based on tacit understanding of the technical challenges that might exist, and also the recognition that there are other components by which additional and/or even paramount considerations need be made. This rubric not only includes areas of expertise required, but the *human* element – whether that is related to competency, aspirations, or potential (see Chapter 3, Career Anchors).

Moreover, the leadership paradigm from the perspective of the technical executive also encompasses both a forward and backward ability to "connect the dots", as well as understand overlaps at the margins; indeed, leading innovation is a key role of the technical executive. Connecting the dots refers simply to being able to recognize relationships from the past which can inform intuition on ones for the future; it is seeing relevant patterns. Similarly, margin overlap of ideas is where one sees potential at areas which may not, at least initially, seem related; examples include (in the past) IT and medicine, or in the product space, "big" data, and paths to country prosperity (see Hausmann et al.). As well, this includes recognizing and responding to disruptive innovation. Disruptive innovation, as described by Clayton Christianson (see, for example, Chapter 6), reflects a novel technology serving a niche customer base, less profitable initially from that of the industry leader, but which may displace an incumbent from its leadership position. Technical executives, who have the unique ability to see and connect the dots and identify overlapping (and potentially unrelated) areas that may be the source of potential future innovations, have a key responsibility for early articulation of these possible threats within an organization. Hence, as noted earlier, the technical executive's leadership abilities are reflected not only in the oft described areas of motivation and communication skills, but also from a core of technical understanding, ability to appreciate other areas of expertise, and being able to both identify appropriate resources (human, informational *etc.*) and other technologies that will fundamentally affect the innovative capabilities within an organization. Figure 2.1 depicts this relationship.

In Ann's case, her inability to understand these components of leadership, despite her detail orientation and execution focus, prevented her from being able

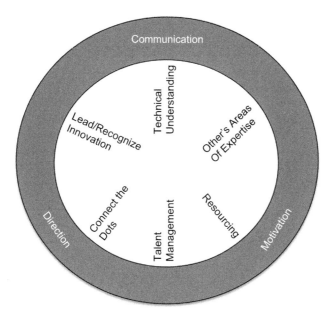

FIGURE 2.1 The technology management and leadership milieu.

to manage and lead; similarly, her supervisor also failed to provide leadership in either communication or direction, thus resulting in a major impact to the organization, with loss of employees, need to hire and train new ones, demotivational activities to both Ann and her subordinates, and no doubt diminished productivity. Leadership training might have been beneficial to both Ann and her supervisor, to clearly articulate a different, broader perspective being required.

"Rank does not confer privilege or give power; it imposes responsibility".

-Peter Drucker

LEADERSHIP IS THE PERSPECTIVE; MANAGEMENT IS THE TOOL

Within the tomes of literature in leadership and management much has been written about the importance of these areas in organizational development and efficiency. However, more recently there seems to be shift to clearly separate the differences between these two areas. In fact, there may even be a moderately derogatory sense about management – we see this in recent quotes and writings: "Management cares about only one thing. Paperwork". (Connie Willis), or "Management, a science? Of course not, it's just a waste-paper basket full of recipes which provided the dish of the day during a few years of plenty and economic growth". (Leon Corville). Similarly, leadership is lauded as the goal of any executive in an organization: "People ask the difference between a leader and a boss. The leader leads, and the boss drives". (Theodore Roosevelt). However, these sentiments notwithstanding, it seems that both leadership and management abilities are needed for the technical executive, particularly sitting in the seat of discovery and development. One advantage of being a scientific or technical professional is the practice one learns early in one's career regarding the identification of a problem. The ability to delineate what is a specific issue is a valuable skill, in that it clears away the less important details in a given situation, and puts forth priorities for consideration and evaluation. The steps required to be considered – while not formulaic – can be thought to relate to the scientific method, applied to the particular area. These might be considered "management", *i.e.* a discipline to carry things out, to measure what can be

System Dynamics: Action in Leadership and Management

System dynamics is a science dealing with describing and understanding complex systems in time, initially developed by Jay Forrester at Sloan School of Management at MIT. Fundamentally, it utilizes internal feedback loops, wherein "stocks" and "flows" change over time, reflecting nonlinearity in processes and results. Often it reveals how relatively simple systems have such nonlinearity, and that this applies to many organizational problems encountered daily. A key aspect of system dynamics is the ability to model complex systems, and create simulations that can help predict outcomes occurring over time. Nelson Repenning and John Sterman, from the System Dynamics Group at Sloan MIT, have shown that despite strong leadership commitment, the management of *process improvement* most often fails as manifest by lack of tangible results. Their findings show that it is not necessarily that the leaders of organizations fail to *choose* the right process improvement techniques, or that management is unable to learn these processes *per se, viz.* it is not the ability to identify or be taught about such methods; rather, it is the *implementation* of these process improvements that reflect the largest challenge. Using a system dynamics approach, they found introduction of any new improvement program cannot be simply a "train and roll out" effort, but must reflect the complexity of interactions between the physical, social, economic, and psychological components of the system. Indeed, management time spent improving *capability* of a process has more enduring change (*even if it does not increase productivity immediately*), than the time spent working *per se*. As well, and not unexpectedly, when one understands the typical nonlinearity of most processes, relatively small actions were found to have large, long-term impacts, particularly when early in the process. By developing a general model to take into account the various system components, and more important, how they interact, system dynamics provide a framework by which management and leadership can be more successful when considering how to execute these process improvements within their respective organizations.

Repenning NP, Sterman JD. *Nobody Ever Gets Credit for Fixing Problems that Never Happened: Creating and Sustaining Process Improvement. California Management Review 42:64–88, 2001.*

measured, and execute on an actionable plan. Leadership might be considered what should be the problem to be addressed; the prioritization of those things that have the most importance for consideration, with the understanding that the resources necessary typically involve other things, notwithstanding the importance, and motivation of, people. As an example, in the area of Neurology, it is often taught that in formulating a case, one follows a path to identify where in the nervous system a problem may lie, the type of pathology which could be the cause, a differential diagnosis, and subsequently by an assessment and plan of attack. Management of this process allows for a plan to be derived for a specific patient, where the consideration of the case includes an entire medical team, where fellows, residents, interns, and medical students work together, led and motivated by an attending physician. While certainly the team can be coerced, the most functional teams work best when armed with a collective goal (which often is the challenge of a particular patient's case, as in this example) spurred on by the encouragement of the various levels of the team. But both the management and leadership are important; we need those who would identify and inspire as much as those who would develop and maintain the *milieu* of the organization. The technical professional can utilize their well-honed analytical abilities to define a problem and approach, applying this to the managerial aspects of their jobs, while understanding the need to motivate, communicate, and direct their respective teams.

Transitions

As seen by Ann's case, the transition from the bench to the figurative management office can be difficult. Not only are there new skills to learn, but the changes in perspective can be a challenge to appreciate, especially as the demands and responsibilities of the new position are manifest. In a parallel manner, it is thus not surprising that moving from the individual contributor role, *viz.* team member, to the one to direct the team (team leader) can be difficult. This can occur at all levels of an organization, and cause confusion to both the team and other management on the role being played by a given individual. Ann's case showed a contributor who was actively attempting to utilize a position title to create a level of self-worth, associated with being in a managerial role; there are other cases when the team leader or manager does the opposite, *viz.* fails to take on the responsibility for directing the team or group. Walt represented such a case.

Walt had a myriad of different experiences in small and large companies, particularly in R&D operational roles. Looking at his annual reviews from all of his past supervisors, in some manner or form, there was always the "such a nice guy" statement. His most current role as a vice president in operations showed how senior managers had come to trust his abilities to get things done. However, when examining his schedule, it was packed with team meetings and calls, and there was considerable time put aside for checking on the results of experiments in his group. In contrast, he only met with his direct reports every two weeks, and each for only half an hour. Both team members and his group always noted that Walt would do anything for the team, but one direct report questioned whether he was being strategic enough, since at one-on-one meetings, he would quote the CEO on corporate goals, without any additional elaboration; his other direct reports seemed happy to have a level of autonomy that was unparalleled in the organization.

Clearly, Walt had not made the transition from team member to team leader or manager, and to an extent had abdicated the role in favor of staying in a comfort zone, which had been apparently successful for him in the past. It is certainly wise for leaders and managers to be willing to do what is needed for the team, and there are excellent lab directors who are able to accomplish this and still provide the motivation, communication, and direction to the group being led. However, as a technical executive, one should be wary when such team or group duties exceed the strategic and tactical considerations of the organization as a whole, rather than the reverse. The role is too important to relinquish, even on a relative basis, for any length of time; while Walt could be a key contributor to the team, the opportunity cost for not being able to lead and manage would have direct manifestations, which would outshadow his other contributions.

"I do not feel obliged to believe that the same God who has endowed us with sense, reason, and intellect has intended us to forgo their use".

-Galileo Galilei

Indeed, Walt needed to consider whether such a management role was appropriate for him, or whether another role would have been more suitable given his prioritization of R&D activities as opposed to managerial ones. In this context, the concept of "internal consultant" or "gatekeeper" has relevance (see Allen and Cohen, References). Despite at times being more senior, these types of "managers" have limited or no managerial responsibility, and actively read the literature and communicate with outside experts on a regular basis. These gatekeepers actively assist others on teams, in groups, at management meetings, and essentially act as internal "key opinion leaders" for an organization; indeed, such individuals tend to be excellent technical performers. Of note is that such individuals cannot be created and can be easily destroyed by management; these are "high communicators" who are not part of a managerial infrastructure, but who are relatively easy to identify, as they are pointed out by others within R&D. These people are incredibly valuable to the organization, with project assignment and execution much more important than supervision duties or title. Senior managers should provide Walt, as well as Cliff (Chapter 1), the option to become gatekeepers rather than managers, and to provide rewards that are meaningful *to them*, such as interesting projects and facilitation roles, as well as salary increases, rather than roles and responsibilities that might not only be of limited value but demotivating as well (such as promotions with increased supervisory responsibility). As a technical executive, understanding whether one is interested in the managerial and leadership role is as important as whether

Evolution of the Gatekeeper: Information *vs.* Knowledge

Since the original description in the late 1960s, the role of the gatekeeper has evolved, primarily because the information sources have both exploded and been more accessible at the same time. Where in the past, receiving and reading the various journals and communiqués in the industry was a gatekeeping function, with search engines, GoogleScholar, Pubmed, and the like, the barrier to access is essentially removed, and the ability to obtain information almost instantaneously when encountering an issue in design or experimentation is fairly straightforward. However, going from the more generic information from web-based or even specialized search engine sources to more specific aspects relevant to the problem at hand can be more problematic. Reliability of information, applicability to the current situation, and understanding of the relationship of the current challenge to the infrastructure of the organization are only some of the encountered issues when accessing information today. Hence, while the gatekeeper in the past was defined more in the context of an information source, today the role has evolved in that such an individual is a *knowledge source*, reflected in the ability to turn the hordes of web links and bewildering arrays of information sources into usable knowledge for colleagues. Indeed, the evolution of the gatekeeper has specifically involved the ability to interpret what sources of information are the most relevant, and, as in the decades before web accessibility was so prevalent, the ability to connect with outside key opinion leaders who can substantiate and elaborate upon information obtained from these sources. Gatekeepers thus now, in addition to the occasional source of information, *validate* the reliability of information using both their knowledge and relationships with the external community, and diffuse and communicate this internally to the relevant infrastructure within the organization.

Harada T. Three steps in knowledge communication: the emergence of knowledge transformers. Research Policy 32:1737–1751, 2003.

one is more satisfied with the gatekeeper role; both are clearly important to the organization, and both have significant influence as a result.

REFERENCES

Allen, T.J., Cohen, S.I., 1969. Information flow in research and development laboratories. Administrative Science Quarterly 14, 12–19.

Hausmann, R., Hidalgo, C., Bustos, S., Coscia, M., Chung, S., Jimenez, J., Simoes, A., Yıldırım, M.A., 2011. The Atlas of Economic Complexity. Center for International Development, Cambridge.

Lunenburg, F.C., 2011. Leadership v. Management: A Key Distinction – At Least in Theory. International Journal of Management, Business and Administration 14, 1–13.

Varma, R., 2000. Research and Development (R&D) Management and Technical Expertise: Creating An Effective Managerial Environment for Maximizing Productivity. Management Development Forum 3, 51–72.

Whelan, E., Ahonen, M., Donnellan, B., 2008. Knowledge Diffusion in R&D Groups: The Impact of Internet Technologies. ECIS 2008 Proceedings Paper 150.

Career Anchors

"De gustibus non est disputandum". (There's no arguing over taste.)

-Anonymous (likely of Medieval origin)

"A professor is one who talks in someone else's sleep".

-W. H. Auden

"The best time to start thinking about your retirement is before the boss does".

-Anonymous

The pace at which the knowledge economy moves has become blindingly quick over a relatively short period of time. This obviously parallels the generation of information, which as noted has been created in the large in the past 30 years. We know for a freshman starting college this year, information will turn over at least once during her undergraduate career, if not more so. As a result, when looking at our options for employment, the expectation is one where we need to be ready to have several types of jobs, probably in a number of different sectors or industries; moreover, we will need to grow within our jobs, with constant education and re-education and learning throughout our careers. While technical professionals to a certain extent are used to constantly acquire new knowledge (reading the literature; going to conferences; attending and giving presentations, *etc.*) the requirements of functional area expertise will be almost by definition insufficient in any organization. The challenge will be to commit to not only learning about one's area of expertise, but other areas as well, and manage oneself appropriately, as a function of one's interest and both organizational and individual priorities.

Managing and Leading for Science Professionals. http://dx.doi.org/10.1016/B978-0-12-416686-8.00003-7

The career paradigm of finding a job one can keep and grow for life based on organizational tools alone will no longer exist; a career will be about effecting choices in a dynamic and evolving job market, which harnesses a multitude of possibilities. Being technically trained will be the beginning but not the end of the education track, and organizations similarly will need to adapt to such needs demanded by stakeholders. Hence, the balance will not only reflect an organization's needs, but the needs of the individual, as the requirements of the *milieu* in which one works will need to be adapted. To a certain extent, this creates the opportunity for individuals to work closely with their organizations to not only match what is needed for the marketplace, but also what is desired by the worker. It provides the technical professional the ongoing opportunity to understand, adapt, and garner both the appropriate as well as the desired skills as he or she moves either within or between organizations.

It is, therefore, important that the technical executive understands the occupational environment, and how it affects careers (both one's own and one's reports). Indeed, the stakes are high. Results from a McKinsey study in India indicated that only about 25% of engineers with bachelor degrees were suitably ready for beginning their careers in multinational organizations. This clearly identifies a need for a careful assessment and understanding of the requirements of the workplace and workers, particularly in technical areas where the degree of change is occurring at arguably the highest rate.

A very useful model for this consideration is the internal *v.* external career paradigm, as initially articulated by Schein (see References). The internal career is the concept of a personal sense of the direction of one's occupational life; it is a subjective idea of where one's work is going. In contrast, the external career is that which is conventionally defined by an organization, including the social and inherent hierarchical structures. The key observation made by Schein and colleagues was that the internal career is one that holds a significant sway, with a strong self-concept despite any changes and alterations present from the external career. Schein coined the term "career anchor" to describe this observation, which has proven predictable toward career choices made by individuals who have been studied over the ensuing decades. Indeed, as articulated, these career anchors are based on not only the self-perceived skills appreciated by individuals, but also the basic values that have been inculcated over the pre-employment and employment years. As well, and potentially most important, is the sense of "motives" and "needs" related to the career – what one wants out of a career, vis-à-vis life in general. Not surprisingly, this is an evolving concept, of which at least initially, one is not particularly aware; this typically will be defined with experience in the workplace and on a personal level. Moreover, we only become aware of our career anchors once we are pressured to make a choice, around family, career, and training/education ("self-development"); the career anchor acts to identify and prioritize our motives and needs, and thus provides a stable point by which we make decisions. As noted, technical executives should be well aware of this concept both from a personal viewpoint as well as one where one considers the people needed to fulfill roles and responsibilities for

TABLE 3.1 Summary of Career Anchors

Career Anchor	Description
Technical/Functional Competence	Regard themselves as "gurus" in an area
General Managerial Competence	Aim is to obtain General Manager title/responsibility
Autonomy/Independence	Solo effort is the aim with lack of reliance on others
Security/Stability	Expects organization will be stable and secure for most if not all career
Entrepreneurial	Drive to create and run an entity which is owned
Sense of Service	Strong desire to work on a particular social service or cause
Pure Challenge	Aim is defined by working on difficult projects which are challenging
Lifestyle	Integrate personal life within working life

the organization. While certainly there are a number of excellent texts regarding team members and roles (see References), understanding career anchors can provide a strong level of self-awareness that can benefit the various members of any team or group.

There are eight categories in which most individuals can be described with respect to career anchors (Table 3.1). Each of these will be considered in turn, particularly in the context of how these relate to anticipated changes in organizations in the knowledge economy. It is of particular note that while there are overlaps in the areas encompassing these career anchors, it is the prioritization of the respective needs and motivations that really tie individuals to particular traits, and when pushed to a choice, they will move and align toward.

TECHNICAL/FUNCTIONAL COMPETENCE

To a certain extent, we have already encountered examples of this career anchor with both Cliff and Walt. In this particular area, individuals with this career anchor see themselves as particular experts in a given area; there is a dominant sense of being highly competent technically. Indeed, these individuals like to be perceived as and covet the title of "guru". Oftentimes they are challenged, as a result of such technical competence, and they consistently perform better than practically anyone else who has attempted the problem. The gatekeepers/internal key opinion leaders often fall into this category (although not all in this category are gatekeepers/internal key opinion leaders). The personal pride that Cliff in Chapter 1 cloned the gene (where others had failed) and the need for Walt to maintain his connection to the R&D function at a very close level suggested anchors to this area. Many who have grown up in the R&D structure necessarily default to this, although there certainly are exceptions. However, the challenge for the technical executive is that while there *may* be the desire to manage to a limited extent, it is only within the functional area, and not in the general management arena; the latter task, unless the executive is adequately prepared, can be fraught with frustration and failure.

Within the rapidity of change, as noted, it will take significant effort to remain an expert with the inherent appropriate training and education to maintain both the title and career anchor. The irony is that with technological change being so quick, the need for experts will increase, but the fact is that obsolescence will occur more quickly than ever. Whether technical executives can continue to maintain the expertise necessary to keep their organizations competitive will reflect their abilities to manage effectively, both at the level of accessing resources for education and training as well as understanding the mechanisms necessary to sustain this career anchor.

GENERAL MANAGERIAL COMPETENCE

Jennifer had received her undergraduate degree in pharmacy, and had joined a pharmaceutical company right out of college. While her initial responsibilities were to provide support for the clinical development team, she spent most of her time interacting with the corporate management group who assigned team leaders for the respective development projects. She became familiar with various managers of both functional areas and matrix team leaders, and eschewed development opportunities within her scientific area, preferring instead to take management courses both internally and outside of the company. When the opportunity arose to become an ex-patriate in England, she jumped at the opportunity to become the first clinical development person in the new office. With the expansion of the office, she was able to hire one subordinate, and she herself directly reported to the site head in London. She lobbied for additional projects to be at least partially executed in the UK, which resulted in both another clinical research associate being hired, as well as a pharmacist to support the teams.

Jennifer's career anchor without doubt revolves around the concept of being a manager; she clearly believes her dominant competence lies in a more generalist role. In this type of career anchor, the individual looks to attain as many experiences and relationships as possible that can allow her or him to attain a general managerial title and/or set of responsibilities. In contrast to the technical/functional competence career anchor, these individuals *desire* a managerial role, which allows them to work across different functional areas with a myriad of different people. While thriving on having responsibility, they can be at times thwarted because of their lack of understanding of emotional intelligence or competence in team dynamics. These individuals may start in the R&D area, and indeed, may rise in the ranks on the functional area side; however, the ultimate goal is to attain a general management position as quickly as possible, where the overall achievement of an organizational goal is a manifestation of the direct actions from the managerial leadership provided. Another challenge for this career anchor is the need to be perceived as and to receive credit for managerial activities; this can be at odds with the need for leadership traits (*e.g.* motivation and direction) in particular projects, creating tension within the team (resulting in demotivating success; see Chapter 1).

Of particular challenge to the technical executive is the need for new skills within this area. However, while this may not be an easy transition, it is also clear that with the level of technical sophistication that programs and projects encompass, there is even greater need for coordination at various (more granular) levels. Hence, both those with the managerial competence career anchor, as well as the technical/functional competence one, have much to learn from one another. Indeed, it has been argued that both areas of career anchor need to be present at progressively lower levels of the organization in a knowledge economy where cross-functional coordination is now a *sine qua non*.

AUTONOMY/INDEPENDENCE

Larry had risen through the ranks of academia quickly, being made an associate professor after only three years and was proposed for full professorship promotion only two years later. While he had published some seminal papers in the area of operations research, he also had expertise in physics, in particular, fluid dynamics. He had obtained funding from both private foundations and government sources, but nonetheless ran a very small lab, occasionally having rotating graduate students, and one technician, who was also his wife. While generous with his time, serving on several thesis committees, he usually was the sole author on most of his research publications, or with one other author (usually a graduate student); he had no publications with other members of his department, although he had been on a couple of other papers from researchers predominantly in industry (in fluid dynamics) where he was considered a key opinion leader. The promotion committee had noted that Larry had only minimal interactions and collaborations with others in the field; however, his external reviews had been so glowing, due to the insights and quality of his work, that it was difficult not to promote him. Moreover, the Dean of the College of Engineering had pointed out that the indirect costs Larry was generating from his grants was significant, and that if he was not promoted, it was most likely the case that he would have many opportunities elsewhere.

Larry was clearly an individual player, with independence associated with a solo effort as a dominant need. Despite being of significant talent and certainly working hard, he found no need to toil in a team environment, or even within the confines of the department, as he had limited participation with others. Larry exhibited a career anchor of autonomy/independence, manifest by working alone, and to a certain extent, outside the bounds of the usual standard rules. His abilities in multiple areas and his seeming lack of need of others within his own work characterize this career anchor. Interestingly, and noted even in the initial technical report by Schein, these individuals are not necessarily introverts; in fact, Larry was quite generous with his time, allowing graduate students to rotate through his lab, and being able to spend time with industry colleagues to help with their research as well. However, when related to his own career, he had his own needs and motivations that did not extend to working with others, allowing him to delineate his work without influence. Such individuals can be quite successful, and also can be gatekeepers/internal key opinion leaders of an organization; however, they can also have significant challenges if forced to work in a team environment, or in any type of managerial capacity. Many of these individuals fail after promotion to positions where autonomy is less available, where collaboration and compromise is an important component. In fact, Larry was made an institute director within his organization, but lasted less than six months, and subsequently departed to another university as a professor with no managerial responsibilities.

Interestingly, this type of career anchor has become more accepted with the level of outsourcing occurring in diverse organizations. For those who wish to remain autonomous, being able to act as a consultant, key opinion leader, or independent business servicing larger organizations meets the needs of many firms allowing the reduction of the expense line on the Profit and Loss statement. Certainly, this maintains both the need for the individual to work independently, and yet participate meaningfully with an organization without either managerial (for the consultant) or employee (for the organization) concerns, resulting in benefits for both parties.

SECURITY/STABILITY

Jeff had worked for the company for over 30 years, in various capacities, culminating in his position as a director of research. He noted that the company had a storied history, and that it would never go out of business. Indeed, he often relayed the story that after finishing school he had sought a large company with significant resources, due to the concern around the recession; while initially, the starting salary was lower than other companies, this strategy had served him well during the economic ups and downs in the ensuing decades. Despite being in a geographic area where there were a significant number of entrepreneurs and start-up companies, Jeff always noted that the risk of these companies was exceedingly high; he did not understand how people who worked either with him or in some cases for him would leave to work for such organizations, and actively counseled against such moves. He proudly wore the company pin on his lapel to outside meetings, and often commented that he had the longest tenure in the department within which he worked. He was unquestioning of policies of the company, from travel to purchasing, and noted the necessity of these for an efficient and well-run organization.

It is almost axiomatic that people need some sense of security within their lives. This is particularly true in times of economic uncertainty, where expectations of stability on income are replaced by the concerns of potentially losing one's job. When this becomes the dominant need and motivation, the career anchor is security/stability. Jeff had a significant sense of need for stability, from the days of the job fair where he had identified his future employer after finishing his formal education. Traits of this anchor include defined goals and expectations, with stability and relative continuity of employment (but not necessarily of position). In this arena, the relative security and stability – for example, financial or geographic – is of paramount consideration, and how all opportunities are defined. When secure in the tenure within a particular organization, there is a high level of loyalty, regardless of the current job or position. Indeed, people like Jeff are more than satisfied in playing "utility infielder", where the role was less important than the association with the company, which provided a significant level of satisfaction. Not unexpectedly, such individuals often spend their entire careers at one company or organization, once the need for security is satisfied. One particular challenge for these employees is that they may be totally shocked if affected by a layoff or strategic change; they may take some time to recover and need additional assistance in finding new work. Indeed, the trends of today significantly affect those with this career anchor, given the lack of certainty of the economic environment, and in turn, long-term employment of any given individual. Even in geographies where lifetime employment was the norm in the past (*e.g.* Japan) or in the public arena (civil service), the changing dynamic has made the idea of long-term tenure an anachronism.

ENTREPRENEURIAL/CREATIVITY

Charlie had come out of academia where he had been both a bench researcher and clinician, joining industry despite success in obtaining grants and achieving the job of leading a division. While he had once noted that one of the greatest thrills was to be the first to see the result of an experiment, during his academic days he still ran a laboratory with two graduate students, three post-doctoral fellows, and a technician, as well as having rotating students and clinical fellows. His medical practice within the hospital included two therapeutic areas, and he served on a number of committees for the medical school. Once he arrived in industry, he continued to consult within his subspecialty area at the local university (pro-bono), and entered into the company sponsored MBA program. He helped in the fledgling therapeutic area group, which was in one of his subspecialty areas, and was asked to volunteer for an assignment in finance to help familiarize the new CFO to the industry. He subsequently left the organization, and started a new company acting as CEO, utilizing a platform he converted into a project paradigm.

Charlie's dominant motivation and need was to create and invent, with the willingness to share the work with those who had either bought into or were part of the vision. In each of the steps of his career, the focus seems to have included some sort of building process, whether that was a lab, a division, or a new therapeutic area within a company. Certainly, there seems to be a bit of an attention deficit to all of the activities noted in Charlie's career progression, but the fact that he had been successful in many of these areas suggests at least a willingness to stick with an effort to overcome obstacles, with promotion to a division head as a result. While this may be similar to individuals who hold the autonomy/independence career anchor, the willingness to work with others clearly differentiates Charlie from Larry as noted above. Interestingly, one of the components of this career anchor is that such individuals often grow bored of their respective jobs, constantly seeking that which allows them ownership, provides an outlet for their creativity, and demonstration of success, usually manifest as relative wealth. As noted, a challenge for this type of career anchor is the perception of being "flighty" or erratic; the search for the principal success may make one appear disloyal.

Interestingly, given the complexity of the economy, those individuals harboring this type of career anchor may be at an advantage. Being creative not only in the development of products, but the business models by which these products or programs are created, will be a significant source of opportunities for not only the entrepreneur but the extended enterprise created and the complementors supporting the endeavor. This career anchor can thus be a driver both for the individual and for a myriad of others who buy into the vision as well as maintain it.

SENSE OF SERVICE

Srinivasan ("Sri") had been an ex-patriate in the USA for two years, working within the software engineering group after being with the company for several years. He was well liked by team members, had a certain bashful charm about him, being soft-spoken even in the most contentious situations. Sri was always cognizant of his family's social situation back home in Bangalore, and had many connections through his USA and India networks to the non-governmental organizations supporting the poor and destitute in his homeland. When the opportunity arose for a software engineer to move back to India, he actively sought the position. However, he noted that with his move back, he wanted to only work part time, and volunteer about half his time to the UNDP (United Nations Development Program) where his skills could be put to use for educating the poor, as well as fighting hunger. While the position was at a higher level than he was at currently, he told the hiring supervisor that he would be willing to work at the same level to ensure his ability to be a part-time employee. Initially, there was resistance to Sri's suggested plan, with the Human Resources Department noting it was against policy to create a new position to replace a currently posted one; however, once it was clear that Sri was not going to alter his position, and that his potential manager acknowledged that Sri could indeed perform the job, the position was modified to create the part-time position, at the higher level.

Sri had a dominant need and motivation to work for the eradication of the social challenges he saw in his homeland. While individuals in this anchor can and do use their skills to help others, their work may be a means to be available to assist in ways which do *not* encompass their specific talents in the occupational world. Sri and others like him have a *modus operandi* to pursue opportunities that help others, often directly, and the value they extract is the satisfaction that whatever they are doing actively makes the world a better place. Such employees can be extremely valuable to an organization, particularly in the context of corporate citizenship and focus, as well as acting as a resource for understanding the impact of its activities globally. Indeed, we see today that those with technical backgrounds like Sri are sorely needed in the developing world, and it is not unexpected that individuals like him will find a need to "give back". Sri's ability to negotiate a solution to the initial policy predicament does not always occur, and organizations need to be cognizant that they could potentially lose excellent employees with this career anchor if unable to be flexible enough to accommodate such needs and motivations.

Today, this career anchor is increasing in numbers. The realization of the challenges of various issues within the world has become more than apparent given the immediacy of media representation of chronic problems such as child poverty to acute issues like earthquakes and tsunamis. The skills available like Sri's create significant opportunity for these organizations to do more than what was ever conceived possible. There are a myriad of firms that can utilize those with this career anchor, which are only increasing daily.

PURE CHALLENGE

Lynn had a reputation for being very intense in personality, which translated directly to her work. While her education was in linguistics, her initial job was in etymology as a field artist; she subsequently had worked as an analytical technician, evaluating the quality of synthetic products, and then subsequently (at another company), as the robotics programmer after teaching herself C++ and FORTH. She was very driven, was always eager to push for perfection, and at times could create solutions to problems that were elegant but unrealistic to implement. Lynn would often volunteer for other projects that were highly challenging, and would work hours either attempting to solve an issue or attempting to learn a skill that might help address a particular problem with which she was working. She often noted that problems "wouldn't beat" the team, and even when an incomplete project was formally ended, would continue to work on the problem until satisfied that she had come up with a solution (often to the frustration of her supervisors). After a little over two years in the robotics position, she applied for and was accepted for a position in the German Country Office to work within the Public Relations Department; while much of the business was done in English, she learned sufficient German prior to her departure to Munich in order to be able to communicate with the German press in their native tongue.

Lynn's career was quite varied, with positions spanning a whole host of different areas. As opposed to the security/stability career anchor, where varied jobs may be a reflection of loyalty to the organization, or the entrepreneurial/creativity anchor, where running an entity dominates, Lynn's history is highly suggestive of the need to seek out challenge *via* difficult problems; indeed, in such individuals, careers can be extraordinarily diverse. Similar to the entrepreneurial/creativity anchor, without such constant stimulation, those with the pure challenge career anchor can often become bored unless having the distinct challenges as noted. As with Lynn's case, such individuals will often challenge themselves to garner new skills with the simple objective of being able to take on new and varied problems that have been identified. It is fascinating to note that many times these individuals have a keen memory to what they have accomplished, and may utilize a wins/losses analogy to describe these activities. The constant stimulation of the challenge – with the diversity and/or novelty that entails – is the end in itself for those with this career anchor. It is obvious that while these employees have a dogged determination for success, they may create risk by continuing to work on projects (and continue to use resources) that have been abandoned for appropriate reasons. While these "skunk works" can be of significant benefit to the organization (*e.g.* in an "ambidextrous organization", see References), they can also create a diversion, which may be less than beneficial. Regardless, it is clear that with the number of programs and projects that tackle some of the most difficult technical problems that exist, individuals with this career anchor will be well-valued by their respective organizations.

LIFESTYLE

Cameron and his wife, Sasha, had always been able to work within the same community, he in the contract manufacturing business, and she in the area of online web design. Several years ago, Sasha made the distinct decision to leave her job in the high-tech area and move into her current role, since she would be able to work from home and care for the couple's two children. At the ages of 8 and 14 years, the boys had seen quite a bit of the world; in fact, two years ago, the family "took off the year" by moving to Australia and travelled throughout both the coastal cities and the outback in order to provide the children a unique experience "before they got too old". While Cameron had worked in the midwest of the USA earlier in his career, this was to accommodate Sasha, who was attending graduate school in Chicago; once she had completed her training, the couple promptly moved back to the San Francisco Bay area where their families resided. Both Cameron and Sasha had turned down promotions that either had

required them to move to new cities, or broadened their responsibilities to the
point where they would be required to travel at least a modicum of the time.
However, they did attend conferences, and would often bring both each other
and the children along. At company outings, such as the summer picnic, both
Sasha and Cameron would take along their extended family, and most of their
respective co-workers both knew and liked these family members.

Cameron and Sasha as a couple had clearly delineated the importance of their family lifestyle as a conscious choice; as a career anchor, the need and motivation was somewhat different than the others in that this was an integration of other areas of life into the workplace. This specifically created a way to encompass the personal needs (of the individual and the family) into the workplace, particularly within a context of a unified whole, rather than separate and at times disjointed parts. The priority and emphasis is integration, and the importance of one's total life is much more relevant than an occupation or job situation; often, this has been referred to as a "quality of life" choice. This type of career anchor can revolve around a number of priorities, such as schools for children, geographic area, and/or spousal work; regardless, the end goal is to achieve an optimal set of circumstances where the integration of career and family can be achieved. Indeed, it is more than a "work-life balance", and reflects an almost seamless integration of career and family life, which requires dedication to preserve. While this may be associated with particular other career anchors, these are specifically subordinated in order to fulfill this lifestyle one. Organizations will need to both understand and adapt to this career anchor, as have members of families, from the days of a single earner who moved to wherever the job took *him*. The reality is that the current *milieu* involves almost always a myriad of different interests with respective needs – spouses, children, activities, geographies, and/or local obligations, all of which earners need account. Those occupational environments and (technical) executives that can best understand and adapt to these interests have the potential to best serve and maintain their employees and the employee pool, respectively, particularly in the context of a dynamic technological and social environment.

It is important to emphasize once again that career anchors may not be readily apparent, at least initially. As noted, both experience and choice need stress the system in order for an inkling as such to be perceived. Indeed, many persons are not aware of their specific career anchors, and certainly, many technical executives themselves have not had the opportunity to evaluate this issue. We as technical professionals often find ourselves at odds with this type of determination, as the diversity of motivations and needs is not an area often discussed in this part of the organization. However, as managers it is incumbent upon us to have a level of self-realization to understand what drives our actions, and the actions of others. By being able to reflect upon these types of issues, our ability to manage others improves. The point is not just to categorize and create prescribed solutions to managerial issues at hand, but rather, to create an archetype where we may be able to explain and enjoin both ourselves and our reports toward more fulfilling work. Career anchors represent a tool to accomplish that goal, helping to facilitate the needs of leadership and management, including those ever important areas such as motivation, empowerment, and communication.

REFERENCES

Kannan, R., 2007. Career Management and Development: The Emerging Paradigm. NHRD Journal 4, 6–9.

Raddon, R. (Ed.), 2005. Your Career, Your Life: Career Management for the Information Professional. Ashgate Publishing, Hants.

Schein, E.H., 1975. How career anchors hold executives to career paths. Personnel 52, 11–24.

Schein, E.H., 2006. Career Anchors, third ed. Wiley/Pfeiffer, New York.

Delegation

"Nothing strengthens authority so much as silence".

-Leonardo de Vinci

"The best executive is the one who has sense enough to pick good men to do what he wants done, and self-restraint enough to keep from meddling with them while they do it".

-Theodore Roosevelt

"The hardest thing in the world to do is to watch someone doing something wrong, and not say anything".

-Anonymous

As noted in Chapter 1, delegation is a key component for the technical executive; it is part of the concept of being able to both develop one's own managerial abilities as well as facilitating the goals of the team and group members. It is qualitatively related to the concept of empowerment in that there requires the transfer of authority (although not of total responsibility) to others within the group, team, or organization. Indeed, one has to be cautious to *not* do the reverse, *viz.* transfer the responsibility but not the authority, a mistake that occurs throughout the management ranks.

DELEGATION: A DEFINITION

However, as technical executives, we often have particular biases about what should or should not be delegated. To be precise, delegation reflects the sharing of a task responsibility with the transfer of the authority of execution to another; it is the clear articulation of both the activity required and the provision of confidence for completion. It is important to consider what delegation is *not*, *viz.* a way to decrease the workload of a manager *per se*, or the deferral of certain activities a manager may be trying to avoid. While there are degrees of delegation (to be discussed) in any decision made by a technical executive, the fundamental tenet is that this is a true transfer of authority and limited responsibility to another, which has relevance to the goals and/or objectives of the organization. This thus requires the technical executive to have some insight into what resources and skills he or she has within the group/team; as noted by many management texts, this reflects one of the key responsibilities of a technical (or other) executive, *i.e.* accessing and hiring the best human resources available that meet the needs of the organization today and tomorrow. It is precisely because of these managerial responsibilities that delegation is so important; as a technical manager, it is simply too difficult to perform all tasks from the bench to budgets, and from human resource development to writing, without involving others. It also clearly requires insight into the technical executive's work style, organizational position, and perspective (see Chapter 3, Career Anchors). Many who have

Sapient – Delegation and Design

Sapient Corporation is an e-commerce solution for many companies, encompassing everything from billing to inventory to marketing and consulting. Created by Jerry Greenberg and J. Stuart Moore, the company has long understood that team empowerment and delegation was an important part of the ethos required in a technologically driven sector. The company is focused around a delegation principle not only impacting decision making, but also encouraging even the most junior member to participate in and be a part of the team and organizational goals. The team structure is very much oriented around an entire industry program or project, where managing directors essentially delegate to teams for all phases.

Indeed, team meetings occur each morning, and these meetings are moderated and led by rotation, including by more junior employees and staff. Whiteboards are used and located everywhere, where work plans, agendas, and more ephemeral notations are written, and where each team member is empowered to write. These team meetings can be motivational as well, where team members are empowered to "manage" others who are in poor spirits.

Finally, there are many "war rooms" for meetings, but no cubicles or "private cabins" for management; the space is typically rows of desks, where both junior and senior members of the office are located. This continues the delegation theme toward team and team members, where the clear objective is success of team efforts, *via* motivation and the ability to work independently but for the collective goals of the team, which are clearly spelled out literally and figuratively.

Sapient India: The Art of Whiteboarding, PR Log, Business Line, May 23, 2011.

Carr DF, Stuart Moore and Jerry Greenberg, Internet World Magazine, pp. 1–4, August 15, 2000.

grown up on the R&D side of the organization will have reticence to give up any level of control of each component of a project, a manifestation of the days in training (see Chapter 1). It may require some practice, patience, and open mindedness for the technical executive to allow members of the group and team to assume authority; a level of trust and open mindedness is often necessary to create the opportunity.

Hence, as defined, delegation is the tangible transfer of authority with responsibility of a given task/operation to another in the organization. It reflects a conscious understanding of the work needed to be performed, and its relationship to the organizational objectives and goals. This transfer thus empowers the delegate to exercise authority in order to fulfill the mission assigned, and to take responsibility for the task at hand.

THE DELEGATION WORK OUT (EXERCISING DELEGATION)

As noted, given the background of most technical executives, the delegation of tasks can be initially problematic. One of the largest issues that has often been identified is to whom delegation is appropriate; what is the context by which delegation should occur? There are a myriad of factors to consider when a technical professional is faced with the new challenges and skills requisite with either a formalized leadership role or a situational one, when considering task delegation. The initial aspect to consider is the delegate – do they have the skills, *or can they develop the skills*, required to complete the task? Obviously, we need to trust our team and group members to be able to perform adequately before engaging within a delegation rubric. However, a key component to this is the capacity for the expanded opportunity; can the individual a technical executive is considering delegating to expand into a role, which they are perhaps not qualified for presently? It is important that, as noted several times, we as technical leaders continue to develop our group and team members so they can grow personally and professionally within the organization. Because we need to have the most relevant human resources we can obtain, this development is not only important for the member of the organization, but for the organization itself. Creating confidence in our team and groups and overcoming fear that we could be mistaken by trusting others is a managerial skill that needs support throughout R&D, and should be facilitated at all levels. Delegation should be practiced over and over again by all executives in order to strengthen this aspect of the firm; if not performed, the atrophy can have significant effects on the group, team, and organizational function with losses of capabilities by demotivation and attrition.

That being noted, a relevant component to this is the *desire of the delegate* for more responsibility and authority. A cautionary tale follows.

Lauren was a graduate student who had been a cytogenetics technician for several years, prior to returning to graduate school to obtain a PhD in genetics. Since there was a member in the department who worked in molecular cytogenetics, she naturally gravitated towards that professor. For her project, she was assigned to work with a post-doctoral fellow, who had already cloned several novel gene sequences and developed, with an industrial partner, new techniques to analyze genomic sequences. The professor/lab director believed it would be of benefit for Lauren to learn and apply newer molecular techniques for her thesis work. While Lauren was quite skilled at isolating the chromosomal pairs from normal subjects, she had difficulty with the more challenging tissues from patients. While the fellow attempted to teach her new techniques, and delegate responsibilities that would encompass her honed abilities and new ones, Lauren focused almost exclusively on her older skills, and spent little time on the novel techniques to which she was being exposed. During lab meetings, she tended to present only the data around these honed techniques, and when queried by the lab director about molecular data, she only noted that those experiments "had not worked". While the fellow continued to try to engage Lauren in newer techniques due to pressure from the lab director, she once noted to a colleague that her interest was only in cytogenetics, and not "those industry things". Lauren and the fellow stopped meeting after about six months, and once the fellow had departed the lab a year later, Lauren was told to continue his work by the lab director. While she did not resist, she herself departed the lab about three months later, to return to her old university job as a cytogenetics technician.

It is important that in our zeal for managerial and leadership excellence to provide motivation and direction that we not forget to assess the individual delegate in the situation. Lauren was clearly skilled, but was uninterested in being delegated additional responsibilities for learning molecular techniques in the lab. One might argue that the fellow did not do enough to motivate Lauren on the rationale or importance of being able to utilize and generate data from these experiments for the entire laboratory's effort, nor the professor's role in this effort; however, the duration and subsequent outcome of Lauren's departure at least suggests a modicum of effort was made. Regardless, it is clear that the determination of a willing delegate is a central role of the technical executive, and a lack of willingness – be it because of competing priorities, lack of desire *etc.* – should be one of the initial considerations when evaluating delegation.

A further consideration on delegation concerns the time for this activity. Many technical (and other) managers have noted constraint of time often limits the ability to delegate responsibly, as attention to qualifications, willingness, and potential for additional responsibility cannot be reasonably assessed. While this may be true, such "fire-fighting" activities at times may be the best time to delegate, if there is some flexibility on outcome. In those situations where it just cannot be done, the better part of valor may be to not delegate and instead directly participate in activities in order to ensure that the risk inherent in the activity is not widened unreasonably (see Chapter 6). Indeed, this was a reason

TABLE 4.1 Delegation Considerations

Qualifications of Individual

Willingness to take on Expanded Role

Ability for Employee to Engage in Task

Available Time for Delegation (both manager and team/group member)

why Gordon Binder, the former CEO of Amgen, participated in the team to pack and ship the erythropoietin product (EPO) 24 hours after approval, due to the need to avoid risk of injunction from a competitor. As a technical executive, combining our understanding of product and project logistics as well as interfacing with our colleagues within other parts of the organization can greatly assist with this determination. See Table 4.1 for those considerations to be evaluated when considering delegation.

WHY DELEGATE?

Delegation empowers both the manager and the individual to whom is being delegated. This is particularly true once the key benefits are understood for delegation. Given that technical managers have as an important responsibility to hire and develop the human resources within their department, utilizing delegation allows them to accomplish this by increasing motivation within their respective groups; this is facilitated by a more involved and engaged workforce, who are empowered to make decisions around the task at hand, knowing they are supported by management. To an extent, it is self-fulfilling in that the engagement obtained when delegating tasks, which have a material effect on goals and objectives of the organization, creates *more* commitment with time, since delegates become more engaged as they are motivated. It is a positive reinforcing loop that revolves around trust and motivations (see Figure 4.1). Moreover, because of the improvement in productivity, costs are reduced, quality is increased, and teams run more efficiently. When teams are more efficient, their creativity can increase, and innovation may improve as well.

The benefits of empowerment by technical executives is also an important consideration. By being able to delegate, the technical executive has presumably been able to develop and/or hire appropriate individuals who can now take on additional responsibility, thereby increasing the manager's own abilities. Moreover, as noted, as the technical professional continues to exercise this managerial muscle, he or she will improve in the execution and preparation of individuals who can contribute to the organization's goals meaningfully and early on in their career or their position. This improves the efficiency of the manager, and increases her or his flexibility with respect to time and effort, particularly

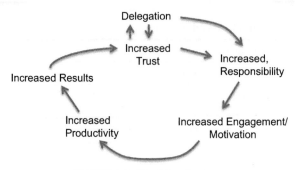

FIGURE 4.1   The delegation loop.

New United Motor Manufacturing, Inc. (NUMMI): Key Factors in Delegation and Empowerment

NUMMI was a plant built by General Motors (GM), initially operated by the company from 1962 to 1982. Subsequently, the plant was closed and then reopened when GM needed a plant to build small cars, at the same time that Toyota decided to build cars within the U.S. The plant, located in Freemont, CA, had a reputation of being the worst plant in the U.S. This was primarily due to the employees – absenteeism, drinking alcohol on the job, passive and active aggressiveness on the cars (with significant impact on quality) was rampant by the workforce. When the plant reopened under a joint program between GM and Toyota, most of the old employees were rehired; many were sent to Japan to learn the "new" manufacturing processes of the Toyota Production System. This system, now well established ("lean" manufacturing), emphasized quality, teamwork, and empowerment; indeed, the plant began producing the most cars with the minimum amounts of defects after these techniques were put in place. Many studies were done on the plant, and revealed that inherent in the Toyota Production System was the emphasis on constant improvement, as well as individual empowerment to stop the line if any employee felt it necessary. The resultant implications were that there was a level of trust between managers and shop floor workers, and that this was noted not only in the ability to halt the line, but also with the training the employees received and the manager's treatment of the workers, within as much as possible the best interests of both. Hence, the delegation of quality to the shop floor employees, and the dedication of all to the concepts of trust, training and best interests, created a situation where a formerly poor running and negative employee environment was converted into the most productive, highest quality plant for GM.

Womack JP, Jones DT, and Roos D. The Machine that Changed the World: The Story of Lean Production. Harper Collins, New York, 1991.

in thinking more strategically about the group or team. By developing the capabilities of the report, the technical executive develops and further enhances the capabilities of the organization and members. This in turn increases the members who can cooperate and improves decision making within the group and across the organization. Hence, the act of delegation improves the manager as it does those who are delegated to, understanding that there is a role to be played by both in the relationship.

SOME TENETS ON DELEGATION

A Word Around Constraints

When technical executives delegate, it typically revolves around specific tasks and/or issues linked to the organizational objectives and goals. This requires, not unexpectedly, clear communication on the goals and the bounds and constraints around the authority provided with the delegated action. In the literature concerning delegation, particularly in science and engineering, it is interesting to note that constraints are actually considered positive. Some see this as a challenge to be fulfilled (a design that accomplishes a goal despite having limitations on resources, profile, capabilities, *etc.*), and/or freedom to operate within a specific tactical environment but not violate the strategy (see Katz, References). Both the direction and clear articulation of the relationship to the organizational goal allow for the team or group to innovate and create a solution having been delegated the task from the technical executive. Again, this emphasizes not only the technical abilities of the team, but the motivational component of the clear articulation of the goal but not the means by which to accomplish it – the team or group is empowered to figure this out. We as technical executives need to resist the temptation to provide a template for the group, but rather let them determine what is needed and come to an approach and solution themselves.

What to Delegate

As noted, one of the key aspects around delegation reflects an implicit or explicit agreement between the technical executive and the team and/or group member on acceptance of the role. While potentially tempting, it is counterproductive to only delegate tasks that are either menial or unpleasant for the manager, and retain those that are more enjoyable. Indeed, we as technical professionals, while certainly appreciating financial rewards, have a strong tendency to want to work on interesting technical projects, which allow us to both utilize and develop our capabilities and expertise. As has been noted elsewhere (see Allen, References), being delegated tasks and programs that have a perceived importance to the organization and where a diversity of tasks are implicit has a positive effect on commitment to the responsibility of accepting delegation. Moreover, we as technical executives should recognize that credibility outside the organization is important as well when we delegate tasks – and that our own role has changed within this context (see Chapter 2).

Hence, there are obviously a wide variety of tasks that can be accommodated when the technical executive considers delegation. Indeed, recent studies show that more conscientious managers tend to delegate more tasks to their respective teams and groups compared to less conscientious managers – this is based on the fact that the former tended to spend time understanding both performance and integrity of their groups, and had a fundamental increased trust (presumably as a result). The tasks considered for delegation should be able to have shared responsibility, understanding that the ultimate responsibility is the manager's, but that the accountability exists in both realms. As such, given an understanding of qualifications, willingness, and timing, broad delegation when teams or team members have shown integrity, and the ability to perform resulting in trust results in the most consistent results in execution, compared to either more limited efforts and/or ones where we as technical executives are less conscientious. Moreover, for those in the executive ranks, making the decision to delegate only when workload is high often results in either micromanagement or undertaking higher risk due to less informed decision making. Hence, when effecting a delegation decision, technical executives should be clear on their own motivations, and have taken some time to understand the potential of the team and group to be able to accept a delegation mandate. Sharing authority and accountability is more facilitated if practiced (rather than rushed or forced) and broadly applicable in a diversity of situations.

Where Can Decision Making Occur?

As technical executives, we are accustomed to trying to ensure that while certain individuals in the group can perform specific functions, it is in the best interest of the lab/group/team that there is overlap in the ability to do a diversity of tasks. Having many being able to perform an experiment with polymerase chain reaction (PCR), or perform a radioimmunoassay (RIA), or utilize computer-aided design/computer-aided manufacturing (CAD/CAM) permits to a certain extent, a minimal reliance and bottleneck on one person to do only specific tasks. While there could be an efficiency argument to divide up tasks in an assembly line fashion, the point is that most on a team or within a group, while having certain specialty areas, can function in general areas as well. Notwithstanding discussions around team designs, one great advantage is this suggests strongly that decision making can move far down into the depths of the organization, limited only by the level of delegation and trust managers have with respect to their team and group members. Technical executives in particular have direct experience in allowing individuals, noting Table 4.1 and issues around performance and integrity, to be able to make decisions about experiments, conditions, and next steps when involved in a program or project. Scientifically, we expect individuals to develop as they make decisions (and mistakes, hopefully followed by successes!), which help them become better technically. By analogy, the same can apply for making decisions at the team level on other project/programs; providing experience in decision making by being delegated responsibility and authority is, as noted, a developmental experience to both the manager and individual being delegated to – pushing this down to the lowest part of the organizational structure possible continuously improves the organization, and as noted, decision-making capability. The more engaged all in the organization are throughout the hierarchy (as such), the better chance that the organization will be productive. Indeed, even in a laboratory environment in academia, programs like those put on by EMBO have been successful in engendering this concept of decision making, all the way to the trainee level (see sidebar, Chapter 1, Principal Investigator as Principal Manager: the EMBO Program).

"Delegating works, provided the one delegating works, too".

-Robert Half

Delegation and R&D: Lessons From Italy

Mediocredito Centrale, an Italian Investment Bank, evaluated the relative link between R&D delegation and productivity by surveying manufacturers in the country in 1997, 2000, and 2003. The hypothesis being evaluated was that less hierarchical, more delegating organizations stimulate managerial incentives, with greater productivity as a result. The results were interesting, in that they found a very significant correlation between delegation of decisions within these organizations with incentives for innovation, and resultant productivity. As well, there was *no* correlation between delegation and the age of companies, the distance from the technological frontier, nor the environment in which the companies operate. As well, there was a *negative* correlation between delegation and "ownership dispersion" – *i.e.* the number of owners of the firm. This study thus shows there exists a positive correlation between delegation and R&D productivity, and suggests that vertical "hierarchical" control is negatively correlated with diffusion of new technologies. While this may reflect the fact that many of the Italian manufacturers studied are either small or family owned, it is fascinating to note that in British and French manufacturing sectors, where the size of the companies is considerably larger, the robust correlation between delegation and innovation is also as robust, suggesting that despite different potential roots of the manufacturing sector, both small and large firms benefit greatly from the ability, at least in R&D, to delegate.

Acemoglu D, Aghion P, Lelarge C, Van Reenen J, Zilibotti F. *Technology, Information and the Decentralization of the Firm. Quarterly Journal of Economics* 4:1759–1799, 2007.

Kasti J, Martimort D, Piccolo S. *Delegation and R&D Spending: Evidence From Italy. Centre for Studies in Economics and Finance, Working Paper No. 192,* October 2009.

REFERENCES

Allen, T.J., Katz, R., 2004. Organizational issues in the introduction of new technologies. In: Katz, R. (Ed.), The Human Side of Managing Technological Innovation, second ed. Oxford University Press, New York.

Kane-Urrabzao, C., 2006. Management's role in shaping organizational culture. Journal of Nursing Management 14, 188–194.

Katz, R., 1994. Managing High Performance R&D Teams. European Management Journal 12, 243–252.

Nicholls, J., 1995. Getting empowerment into perspective: a three-stage training framework. Empowerment in Organizations 3, 5–10.

Hakimi, N., 2009. Leader Empowering Behavior: The Leader's Perspective. ERIM PhD Series in Research Management 184.

Taking Interest: New Skills

"The main ingredient of stardom is the rest of the team".

-John Wooden

"We must all hang together or most assuredly we shall hang separately".
-Attributed to Benjamin Franklin (probably apocryphal)

"A successful man is one who can lay a firm foundation with the bricks others have thrown at him".

-David Brinkley

Dr. Karla
Karla had been in academia for several years, predominantly in a clinical practice associated with the local cancer institute. She joined a new pharmaceutical company in order to design clinical trials for the development of a promising new therapy that was just progressing through preclinical stages and was to enter the clinic shortly. Karla helped with the design and execution of the initial studies, which showed benefit for patients with certain types of cancer. This required the company to grow; as a result, she hired two additional clinicians, who were also skilled in oncology. Despite rising in the company with its success, she spent most of her time scrutinizing the work of her reports, and insisted on not only review of the clinical protocols but all publications, the latter of which she always made herself senior

43

author. Her policy was that any presentations about company data were to be made by her, unless driven by an external investigator; while her subordinates were allowed to interact with key opinion leaders in the community, this was to be done with her present. Within her first year, Karla had lost one of the clinicians on her team, and the other clinician had threatened to leave. She was transferred to another part of the organization that was more focused on interacting with external investigators, while a new director took over her previous responsibilities. In her new position, she then hired three additional clinicians, one having just finished his training, and the other two who were more experienced. The latter two physicians left the company relatively shortly thereafter, one noting the "oppressive atmosphere" within the department.

It has been noted that technical executives tend to have a level of need for individual accomplishment and control, from the days in training (see Chapter 2). Karla, it is presumed, had not had any managerial experience prior to arriving in industry, with her primary experience being patient care in an academic practice. Unfortunately for her reports, she continued to treat the company similar to some academic settings, where those who are more senior expect to receive a level of credit in various forms, including publications, due to their status alone (this has changed significantly with respect to authorship on publications, and today would not have been permitted). Karla continued to expect and needed to have the attention focused on her efforts, despite her and the company's success and requirement therefore to bring in new employees. This necessitates a significant change in behavior often needing to be addressed as technical executives, *viz.* it is no longer about ensuring recognition of our respective efforts; it is actually much more important to recognize and empower our groups/teams, rather than to use any authority we might have to self-aggrandize. The reasons are clear from earlier discussion – motivation, empowerment, development of the entire organization and the delegating manager, *etc.* – are all relevant within this context. But it can be quite difficult to step away from this need – it takes a conscious effort to pull away from an almost natural tendency to want and accept praise. However, for the technical executive, as many management books have noted, and from previous discussions herein, this can be demotivating and create significant hostility between individuals and groups as a result. A particularly relevant concept is that one *must* change from being concerned about one's own career/data/experiments to that of the group or teams' – this is the responsibility of management to facilitate these efforts. The need for the manager to "get credit" for efforts in areas within which we are responsible does not engender a positive working relationship within the organization – as an individual who has been promoted, the organization has already recognized our competency; we need to push that competency down into the organization as far as possible. Hence, acknowledging the efforts (and successes) of our groups is a paramount responsibility of technical management.

"A good leader takes a little more than his share of the blame, a little less than his share of the credit".

-Arnold Glasgow

DEFINING THE TECHNICAL EXECUTIVE ROLE

It has been discussed that the role of the technical executive is to provide facilitation of the goals of the team, in a variety of different ways. However, it is equally important that the technical professional minimally begins to conceptualize strategically about his/her area(s), vis-à-vis the organizational needs and objectives. To be sure, each technical executive in charge of a group or team should ensure that there is a clear and granular understanding about the strategy

Building Strategies: University of Bolton Strategic Plan 2006–2012

As an organization, the University of Bolton, located in the Northwest region of England, has created a strategic plan that outlines its proposed role as a university, *viz.* "a community of professionals committed to developing other professionals" as articulated by their strategic plan. This was a particularly important task, as the school had changed from being an institute (Bolton Institute) to achieving university status, beginning to grant degrees in 1995. Like most strategic plans, it encompasses external realities of competition and revenues (e.g. other universities, training programs, and student fees, with the changes in public funding) as well as changing demographics and aging of the population (accessible client base). Within this context, the university as a whole articulated the primary strategic goal (broken down into five sub-goals) to be both global and local, and to service professional needs of students as much as possible (hence, the moniker "University of Bolton: The Professional University"). However, this still needed to be within the framework of the maintenance of the identity as a local organization supporting local students. On the departmental level, supporting plans were put in place in order to clearly match with the overarching goals of the university. By 2009, the university published its interim review of the strategic plan. As example, both the university and individual departments have a presence within the local community, supporting both full-time and part-time students, given the needs of both traditional and working students. The university had expanded overseas, with campuses in China and Dubai/UAE in order to develop upon its global mission. There has been the establishment of liaison programs with industry in institutes such as the Centre for Materials Research and Innovation as well as the Business School, and ongoing interactions between the schools of the university and departments with local and international industry groups to maintain programs as relevant and up to date as possible. While strategic activities and tactical execution continue for the university, the importance of being able to translate the overarching strategy to a school and departmental strategy is clearly important to realize the objectives and goals of the university as a whole.

University of Bolton Strategic Plan 2006 – 2012, Vice Chancellors Office.

and objectives of the organization, and how this translates to his/her larger division and subsequent department or group (see sidebar, Building Strategies: The University of Bolton Strategic Plan, 2006–2012). It is often a mistake of technical managers to be much more involved, to the exclusion of strategic thought, around the tactics occurring within the group or team, rather than having a firm understanding that their role is a translating one. Managers need to consider how each strategy of the company can be implemented into the division/group/department as one that addresses the ongoing activities within the technical area; this includes not only the projects and programs ongoing, but the development of group/team members to fulfill needs within the organization, interface with other parts of the firm, and support (as necessary) of the concurrent commercial activities. Hence, not only is the facilitation role important within the technical executive's responsibility, the need to move the organization's overall strategy into strategies for the part of the organization of which he/she has accountability is another tantamount objective. Clearly, this level of activity, in addition to the usual supervisory role a manager plays, is a strong rationale for the development of personnel within the group by empowerment and delegation, in order to improve decision making and allow the manager to fulfill her/his other responsibilities to the organization.

ACTIVE LISTENING

As busy technical executives, having to learn new skills (such as managing persons potentially for the first time), simultaneously trying to maintain a modicum of competence at the scientific, engineering, or other technical level, paying "enough" attention to each to allow programs, projects, or just day-to-day activities to move forward can be extraordinarily challenging. While reading the abstract and the material and methods section of a paper (rather than the whole manuscript) or skimming the executive summaries at the end of the *MIT Sloan Management Review* to identify only the articles to delve into at some other time can be time efficient, one area that often needs *further* enhancement is the skill of active listening. As noted, when busy with various high priority activities, it is easy to become distracted and not fully engaged, particularly when we are speaking with colleagues and subordinates; this is particularly true in technical areas, where we might have a specific point of view regarding the interpretation of data and/or the next set of experiments to perform. Often we are focused on a response rather than listening; this is particularly true when we might not fully agree with what is being said, and have dismissed what the speaker's point might have been. This can obviously lead to erroneous conclusions and potential downsteam effects having important consequences. In contrast, active listening really focuses attention on the speaker; it directs our concentration on understanding the speaker both in content and tone; it requires the confirmation of what is being said to avoid misinterpretation. This provides an opportunity for the speaker both to elaborate and clarify, in order for the listener to fully grasp what is being said. By actively listening, a relationship can strengthen based on respect, rapport, and trust. It is no wonder that in negotiations and conflict resolution, the use of active listening has been associated with being able to develop better solutions to problems, rather than using contradictory statements that are responded to defensively.

There are a number of techniques used for active listening (see Table 5.1). These can be used in a variety of different ways to better understand the articulation

TABLE 5.1 Techniques in Active Listening

Technique	Concept	Example
Restating	Demonstrates listening is occurring by paraphrasing speaker	"What I am hearing you say is…"
Summarizing	Summarize after a number of points are made	"Let me see if I understand your points…"
Providing feedback and encouragement	Give feedback based on understood material; use open-ended statements to encourage speaker	"My thoughts are…; what are your additional thoughts/ideas/ understandings?"
Identify emotions and reflecting	Create context on statements being made	"This is clearly important to you…I sense your level of frustration…"
Probing	Obtaining and allowing more granularity for the speaker	"Are you thinking that…"
Silence	Provide potential for both emphasis and/or engagement; can be used especially to slow down or focus a point	
Validation	Acceptance of a given point or concern	"It's clear that this is a particularly important issue to you/your firm…"
Redirecting	Moves the discussion to another area or topic, particularly when emotionally charged	"Let's talk about…"
Consequences	Identify in a nonthreatening way potential consequences; potentially offer your experiences (if asked)	"Do you have experience when XYZ has occurred…in a similar situation [describe] we have seen…"
Gathering more information	Specifically ask for more data based on speakers statements	"That's interesting; what else have you seen…"

of the speaker, and encourage additional dialogue. Many of these techniques can be applied to a number of situations depending on the context, but it is important to understand that just using a few of these will enhance understanding and contribute to a better relationship with the speaker.

These are just a few of the potential techniques that can be used; there are additional writings within the references both expanding upon these and identifying other ways to actively listen. One last point is to avoid those actions that inhibit or stifle communication; these can not only erect barriers during an interpersonal interaction, it can tear down the work that was built up by active listening in the first place! Examples of these include interruption (lack of interest), preaching (lack of respect), dismissiveness (*e.g.* "Don't worry about that"), advising (without being requested) (tends to end interaction), patronizing ("I know how you feel"), or stealing the show ("You think that's bad; when it happened to me..."). Particularly as a more senior person, the technical executive must be attune to understanding that being articulated, and that being implied. Only by active listening and avoiding communication blockers can we hear what is being said.

KNOWING ENOUGH NOT TO BE DANGEROUS

In addition to the new skills required of the technical executive, it is clear as noted that there is a new set of responsibilities for acquiring not only technical knowledge, but more general management knowledge as well. Certainly, this provides two specific aims: the first is a general familiarity with terminology used to describe business processes, and the second, to garner a better understanding of what priorities often exist at the managerial level of the organization. There are some excellent texts encompassing such aspects, of which only a sketch will be presented here. Nonetheless, it is clear that in order to facilitate communication (a theme throughout this book; see Chapter 9), at least some conceptual parallels should be understood.

Corporate Strategy

Corporate strategy has been mentioned previously, although not particularly defined. While there are many definitions of corporate strategy, a convenient one is the approach a business takes to achieve the company's long- and short-term objectives. As noted in the vignette above on the University of Bolton, the "corporate" strategy revolves around the university, and the objectives are to be able to service local and global constituents ("customers"). Within this vein, the organization is approaching its "business", and as noted, the components of the business should reflect the mechanism by which these objectives can be fulfilled. Hence, the idea of corporate strategy is to provide direction; the divisional or departmental strategies (*e.g.* human resources strategy, operations strategy, R&D strategy, *etc.*) should support this direction in the particular ways appropriate to their respective areas. The manner by which these departmental or divisional strategies are accomplished are by *tactics*, *viz.* the actions that follow the strategies. There are a number of corporate strategies that have been articulated commonly in use by organizations (*e.g.* Five Forces Model, Boston Consulting Group Business Portfolio Model, Delta Model, Resourced Based View, *etc.*); all focus on the business of the organization, and are complementary in the view to achieve value. To summarize, the corporate strategy articulates the way the organization will accomplish its objectives; each department/division will have its own strategies reflective of and supporting these corporate strategies, which will be manifest as tactics.

Strategy: A Sports Example

There are a variety of ways to depict strategy, particularly using military analogies. However, sports also provide a perhaps more understandable way to look at the formulation of strategy and how it can inform how to "play the game", whether that be an athletic or organizational question.

In tennis, there are a variety of styles that can be used during play. As example, there is the aggressive player, who attacks all of the time, or the player who puts an incredible amount of spin on the ball on every shot. Then, there is the player deemed "the human wall", who returns every ball, not really very hard, or with very much spin, but just is able to get the ball over the net very frequently, and only rarely is aggressive in attacking. The *objective* is to play on the fact that he does not hit the ball hard, albeit he returns most from the back of the court. There are several *strategies* that can potentially unseat this kind of player; one can be aggressive, attacking the net, knowing that while he may be able to hit the ball back, it will not be particularly hard and be quite playable; the *tactic* may be to serve and volley. Another *strategy* is to play the "waiting game" since he cannot overwhelm with his shots; here, the *tactic* would be to wait for one of his shots that can be attacked or used to approach. A final *strategy* would be to make him hit shallow shots, which can then be approached more easily; the *tactic* would be to hit topspin balls to the backhand side, which can be difficult to hit back deeply. Hopefully, one or all of these strategies can be used in order to reach your *goal* to win the match!

   Gilbert B, Jamison S. *Winning Ugly. Fireside, New York, 1993.*

Marketing

Marketing represents an important part of any organization providing value to customers, manifest by the activities and processes effected to access, communicate, and deliver this value. Within a technically oriented organization, the ability to anticipate the technologic needs of the customer often creates a competitive advantage vis-à-vis other suppliers. Arguably, it is thus the relationship between the technical and marketing functions within an organization that

TABLE 5.2 Marketing Mix

Product	Offering that solves a problem for a customer; also includes Service
Place	Distribution channel of the Product by which it moves from manufacturing to the customer
Promotion	Product attributes and value proposition communicated to the customer
Price	Value exchanged from customer for Product

creates the most significant value by being able to both anticipate and create technology fulfilling customer wants and provide a mechanism for customers to access these solutions. Indeed, Souder (see References) showed that a "harmonious" relationship between marketing and R&D resulted in most projects succeeding commercially, whereas "disharmonious" (*viz.* silo) relations between the two functions resulted in projects that failed *five times more frequently*. Some terms that could be encountered: a *market* is a group of customers that may be interested in a product/service; a *market segment* is a subset of the market that can be targeted, for example, with a marketing mix. This *marketing mix* (often referred as the "four Ps"; see Table 5.2) encompasses the areas of product, place, promotion, and price. Products can be thought of as those items that solve a problem for a customer; the way by which products move to the customer is the distribution, or place, of the product; promotion refers to the communication of the product attributes and the value proposition to the customer; and the price reflects the exchange of the offering of the organization for some value. While tightly intertwined, marketing should be distinguished from sales; marketing reflects those activities to reach and persuade prospective customers, while sales (the sales process) includes aspects that close the sale resulting in a purchase, signed agreement, or contract.

Finance and Accounting

Finance and accounting help in determining and planning the use of resources within an organization, and provide a common language for such understanding. In general, there are two types of finance that are important to consider: financial accounting and managerial finance. Financial accounting relates to the evaluation of the organization during a defined period, and is a retrospective evaluation typically for external parties such as investors and analysts; this is the type of accounting that uses generally accepted accounting principles (GAAP). In contrast, managerial finance is used for internal decision making, and allows for planning of resources for the future, based on the input of executives (including technical) inside of the organization; hence, this type of effort is much more inwardly focused. The financial statements that are often discussed revolve around the balance sheet, the income statement, and the cash

TABLE 5.3 Communication Vehicles in Finance and Accounting

Balance Sheet	Snapshot of the organization, reflecting assets and liabilities
Income Statement	Reflects the results of Operations over a period of time
Cash Flow Statement	Uses and sources of Cash by the organization over a period of time

flow statement. The balance sheet is a snapshot of the organization, which shows the assets and liabilities at a specific time; assets reflect that which the organization owns (or has claim to), and liabilities reflect obligations to pay or deliver something of value in the future. Another term within this context is shareholder equity; this reflects the accounting estimate of the shareholder value of investment in the organization. The income statement refers to the revenues brought into the organization over a period of time (*e.g.* a year); it shows the result of operations, based on profits or income. Finally, the cash flow statement identifies the principle sources and uses of cash within an organization. Similar to the income statement, this is typically assessed over some time period. Table 5.3 summarizes these concepts.

General Terms in Economics

Inflation is of obvious concern for any organization; it is the rise of prices associated with a relative increase in money supply compared to demand. The key for technical executives to note is that higher inflation reduces the overall value of capital at the expense of the lender; similarly, lower inflation benefits the lender, as the value of money is higher. Because the U.S. government is the largest debt holder in the world, there is a tendency for higher inflation.

Exchange rates are important due to the globalization of many of our organizations today, manifest by sales abroad or accessing raw materials or labor overseas. Monetarily, exchange rates merely reflect the value of one currency expressed in another; there are several ways to make the comparison, although the "spot" and "bilateral" exchange rates are the most common. The spot rate refers to the exchange rate at current market prices, and varies related to the flow of supply and demand for the currency; the bilateral rate refers to the comparison of two currencies directly (*e.g.* euro/dollar). The governments of countries can vary these rates, based on the action of central banks buying and selling currencies, which can thus affect prices both domestically and abroad.

The supply and demand concept is from microeconomics, *i.e.* the study of individual units of an economy (*e.g.* individuals, households) and their behavior. Supply and demand reflects the interaction between the suppliers of product/services and the demand for such services; this thereby determines price. An equilibrium can be determined in supply and demand at a given price

Not Enough Coin: Using U.S. Dollars in Zimbabwe

Zimbabwe in the past was subject to huge inflation; any cash transaction literally took boxes of currency to complete. Estimates vary, but at one point the inflation rate was 2,600% per *month*, which translated to an annual inflation rate of about 231 million % per year. The cause of this *hyperinflation* (which is commonly defined as a 50%/year inflation rate) was the governmental policy of printing currency to suit its own needs (*e.g.* paying bills). In January 2009, the country was printing bills worth 100 trillion Zimbabwe dollars, which could not even buy a loaf of bread.

That same year, after much pressure, the government adopted the U.S. dollar as the official currency. This stabilized the monetary system, virtually wiped out inflation, saved the economic system, and allowed some growth to occur. The difficulty is that while dollars are being used, the currency is of high value, but there is little change in the form of coins, due to the fact that coins are heavy and are expensive to ship to the country. Hence, when purchases are made, there is often no change, requiring replacement items like candy, pens, or matches to make up the difference. The lack of confidence in the government, or government issued monetary instruments (cash, coins, or other notes) puts the burden of cash management on consumers and merchants, where the exchange rates between any amounts less than a dollar translate to tomatoes, clothespins, onions, or steel bottle openers, to name a few items.

Polgreen L. Using US Dollars, Zimbabwe finds a problem: No change. NY Times, 25 April, 2012.

and quantity to be supplied to the marketplace; this equilibrium can change when either/both supply and demand change, thus changing price and quantity required. This assumes that increases in demand are associated with an increase in price if there is a constant supply, and that lower demand with the same constant supply will result in a decrease in price.

Quality Management

Referring to management operations, quality management is an important aspect for the technology executive to understand, as the ultimate output of product development is the manufacture and sale to an end user. This encompasses the avoidance of waste, efficiency of production, and implementation of programs designed to achieve highest total quality. This needs to be an organizational commitment at all levels, rather than just one from the manufacturing part of the organization, toward adherence to processes and products at the highest level of quality. Indeed, quality is reflected within the efficiently produced products with well-designed processes, to that which meet consumer needs. Estimating resources necessary for quality costs includes appraisal costs, prevention costs, internal and external failure costs. Lean manufacturing is a concept derived from the total quality management approach, wherein the elimination of waste, manifest by consistency of operations, decreasing complexity of process flow, and minimization of variation. Finally, six sigma is another term of which to be familiar within this context; it represents the statistical aspects of process capability improvement, emphasizing the prevention of defects – such quality performance is to the point of no more than 3.4 defects per million iterations, and similar to other total quality management approaches, relates to reduction of variability and waste.

Deadly Results in Loss of Quality

In mid-September 2012, an astute clinician in Tennessee reported a case of fungal meningitis in a patient with a normal immune system, a very rare occurrence. The patient had received an injection of steroids in the space around the covering of the spinal cord ("epidural injection"). The steroid was obtained from a compounding pharmacy, which combines and/or mixes different ingredients of drugs by a licensed pharmacist to produce a drug specific for a given patient or clinic's needs, based on a prescription from a medical practitioner. However, unlike brand name and generic drugs, these compounded drugs are not evaluated by the Food and Drug Administration (FDA) and thus do not receive the scrutiny around manufacturing the former do; states are responsible for the licensing of such pharmacies within their borders. This patient finding prompted an investigation by the Department of Health, who found two other patients who had received similar injections at the same clinic had also contracted meningitis, but (at the time) of unknown cause. The clinic was investigated and revealed no etiologic causes for these cases. By the end of September, eight patients had been identified with meningitis who had received epidural injections of steroid from the clinic. Further investigation noted that the steroids were obtained from a single pharmacy, the New England Compounding Center, in Framingham, MA (NECC). After obtaining distribution records from NECC, the FDA obtained samples from previously unopened vials of the steroid; evaluation revealed that there was fungal contamination from these materials from NECC. The FDA then inspected the facility where the compounding of the steroid was performed. There were a number of quality failures noted; the clean room was found to be contaminated, as was the adjacent transition room; the air conditioners were not running throughout the night, which was standard operating practice to maintain humidity and temperature control; and there was foreign material in some of the vials of the injectable steroid. The conclusion from the Bureau of Health Care Safety and Quality at the Massachusetts Public Health Department was that there were "significant issues with the environment in which medications were being compounded", with a total failure of quality and systems controls for pharmaceutical grade products. The result has been that over 30 people have died who received the tainted product, and over 400 become ill. It is estimated that over 14,000 patients may have received steroid injections of material from NECC.

Kainer MA et al. Fungal Infections Associated with Contaminated Methylprednisolone in Tennessee. New England Journal of Medicine, November 6, 2012.

Portfolio Management

Many technical professionals recognize portfolio management as the component projects that exist within the pipeline of the firm, typically in R&D; these reflect the programs that need to have resources prioritized in order to ensure the pipeline has the appropriate balance between various programs of different stages for the marketplace. However, portfolio management at the corporate level has broader reach than this; it is not only the programs and projects within the technical part of the organization, but also activities that affect both needs of and value opportunities for the firm. In addition to the product portfolio, part of the corporate portfolio could be manufacturing plants, identification of off shore resources for sales and marketing, and/or creation of a new business unit *etc.*; indeed, despite this seemingly large variation of items within the portfolio, all should allow for creation of value for the firm; it is the interaction of all components of the corporate portfolio to create true synergies within the firm that gives the most opportunity. As such, connections to the corporate strategy, and the derived divisional and departmental strategies and tactics, are of paramount consideration to effect the greatest impact. This is seen in the operational performance of the organization, manifest not only by the external achievements (*e.g.* revenues) but also the internal ones (*e.g.* development of capabilities). Tools such as decision analysis, real options and/or portfolio optimization (on which many consultant firms are more than happy to advise and assist the organization) can facilitate the process.

Product Development

Almost by definition, technical executives are familiar with the development of products as the mainstay or result of their respective efforts. In addition to the usual stages of development on the R&D side, there are also marketplace product development paradigms of which the technical executive should be familiar. These are important, as the different stages of a commercial product impact the nature of the portfolio (see above) with considerations on keeping offerings from the organization consistent, as constant as possible, and dedicated to the overall business of the firm. Within this context, is the product life cycle, which provides a useful manner to think about how products move through the marketplace; while not all products move through the product life cycle for various reasons, it allows an understanding of the challenges faced for products or services upon launch. Generally, the four stages of the product life cycle are introduction, growth, maturity, and decline. In the introduction stage, a product is launched that has not been previously on the market; profits are none to low, and uncertainty is high. The growth stage reflects more awareness of the product; there are increases in sales and profits, competition ensues, and profitability is the highest during the latter part of this stage. In the maturity phase, sales begin to flatten, and while this phase may last a significant amount of time, there is high risk of new products emerging or changes in dominant design (see

TABLE 5.4 Product Life Cycle

Stage	Components	Profitability
Introduction	Not previously on the market; adoption risk	Losses
Growth	Increased awareness; beginning of direct competition	Highest at end of stage
Maturity	Plateau of sales; concern with emergence of replacements or changes in dominant design	Decreasing
Decline	New technologies available; shakeout based on cost constraints	Low (but potentially stable for some time)

Chapter 6). Finally, in the decline phase, there is another product that is superior in the marketplace, and there is a reduction in sales and profits. Costs are key in this point of the product life cycle, and only those with the most efficiency will survive (*viz.* a "shakeout" occurs). Profits are low, but may be consistent; the end of this stage for the organization is either upon withdrawal or being sold to another manufacturer. Table 5.4 summarizes these components.

Within the product development life cycle, the technical executive will be exposed to "disruption", or "disruptive innovation"; this refers to the ability of smaller firms with (initially) lower quality products displacing a larger company's dominance (mentioned above in the maturity phase). These latter products typically serve a niche customer base that is less profitable (and thus often ignored by the industry leader); however, gradual innovation from the small company, unimpeded by a larger company, results in a gradual improvement of the product, which can eventually displace the incumbent from the leadership position. As technical executives, a key responsibility we should be highly qualified for is to identify these potential disruptive innovations, and recognize early the level of threat these products might engender; approaches to stave off such dangers can be implemented in order to prevent further market share gains.

REFERENCES

Christensen, C.M., 1997. The Innovator's Dilemma: When New Technologies Cause Great Firms to Fail. Harvard Business Press, Boston.

Newman, R.G., Danzinger, M.A., Cohen, M. (Eds.), 1987. Communicating in Business Today, Heath & Company, Lexington, D.C.

Rogers, C., Farson, R., 1979. Active listening. In: Kolb, D., Rubin, I., MacIntyre, J. (Eds.), Organizational Psychology, third ed. Prentice Hall, New Jersey.

Souder, W.E., 1988. Managing relations between R&D and marketing in new product development projects. Journal of Product Innovation Management 5, 6–19.

Risk = Management (as does Uncertainty)

"A man who procrastinates in his choosing will inevitably have his choice made for him by circumstance".

-Hunter S. Thompson

"So what do we do? Anything. Something. So long as we just don't sit there. If we screw it up, start over. Try something else. If we wait until we've satisfied all the uncertainties, it may be too late".

-Lee Iacocca

"Human beings, who are almost unique in having the ability to learn from the experience of others, are also remarkable for their apparent disinclination to do so".

-Douglas Adams

The Need for Certainty Avi had been a middle manager in product support for the company for several years, after working in engineering and design. He was known as a methodical employee and sequentially organized his day-to-day activities related to the projects having the highest priorities at the time. He worked well with team members within the group, and was able to anticipate potential challenges in programs and address them with the relevant team members both on the commercial and technical sides of the business. Avi would either patiently or tirelessly attempt to obtain data and information regarding

Managing and Leading for Science Professionals. http://dx.doi.org/10.1016/B978-0-12-416686-8.00006-2

every aspect of his set of responsibilities, documenting these carefully in differentially colored folders on his desk; he once noted this level of organization was an approach derived from both his engineering days and the way he worked on the "squawks" (problems) on his 1948 Piper Cub airplane – "you don't get to make mistakes up there!". In spite of this, Avi had been passed over several times for promotion within the product support group. His supervisor had noted that while he was an excellent team member, and that his 360° feedback was uniformly positive with his technical brethren, it was only mediocre with his commercial colleagues. The latter complained that while complete, responsiveness was relatively poor from Avi, manifest by "at times unreasonable" delays in both internal and external requests. Avi was puzzled, in that such criticism was not noted by those within the product development, product support, or engineering groups. Why the difference?

RISK AND UNCERTAINTY

It is important to both define risk as well as uncertainty, to be more precise on what types of consequences are being evaluated. While there are a number of ways to define risk, an established and accepted paradigm from the University of Chicago economist Frank Knight is based on probability. In this rubric, there are three types of probability to be considered. This includes *a priori* probability, reflecting *mathematical probability* (*e.g.* chance of rolling seven with a dice); the second is *statistical probability*, which is based on empirical circumstances; an example of this is assessing the rate of out of specification product in manufacturing; and the third is the concept of *estimates*, wherein when there is "no valid basis of any kind for classifying instances", only an estimate can be made. Risk, within this set of concepts, relates to the first two, and uncertainty to the last. Thus defined, risk relates to choice that can be at least informed (if not guided) by probabilities, while uncertainty can be thought to reflect a situation where the data is too imprecise to be described by probabilities (summarized in Table 6.1).

TABLE 6.1 Definitions of Risk and Uncertainty

Risk	Example
A priori (mathematical) probability	Chance of "heads" when flipping a coin
Statistical probability; empirical	Material specification variability
Uncertainty	
Estimate; no statistical description applicable	Uptake of "lite" beer in Hungary

For the technical executive, this is an important distinction, since in certain circumstances (as pointed out by Knight) business decisions can and usually are incredibly unique; indeed, these estimates are almost speculations – despite any market research or Monte Carlo simulations, they are not based on any statistical inferences either mathematically or statistically defined. Moreover, on a system dynamics basis, the assignment of risk and uncertainty also revolves, at least at the organizational level, on the cultural aspects of the respective firm, and hence decisions can be framed within not only the presence or absence of different types of probabilities, but also how the organization is perceived by its managers (and the acceptability – or not – of risk and uncertainty). Commonly, we assume that certain types of organizational decisions will fall into one or the other category; however, the important consideration is that in risk, there may be a particular level of information that can be defined and assessed, boiled down to and summarized by a given probability component. However, uncertainty, in distinct contrast, which as noted encompasses a fair number of business decisions, does not have that level of definable probability, and the situations are so distinctive that additional information adds at most incremental data to the situation. Both these concepts are important to technical professionals, and to individuals like Avi, who may have had difficulty with decision making.

RISK, UNCERTAINTY, AND DECISION MAKING

There have been many studies that revolve around decision making from a psychological, economic, social, and business perspective. A number of heuristics have been used, many which seem contradictory when considering how and why individuals choose to act in certain ways. Indeed, decision making particularly in business, reflected as economic or economically related decisions, are often made conceptually (*i.e.* "from the gut"), and relate to either "risk-prone" or "risk-averse" perspectives. Interestingly, these are not entirely consistent, depending on the context. Not unexpectedly, the reaction to risk and uncertainty is to avoid it, and many studies show that managers tend to bear these in an adverse way. However, even understanding this, most managers believe that accepting risk/uncertainty is necessary, and that it is clearly related to return. Interestingly, most managers, even those with some decision-making experience, will react "consistently inconsistent" in situations with the same or similar economic values, depending on framing. To wit, they will have *risk averse* tendencies for *positive* situations (*e.g.* choose a guaranteed lesser amount, rather than a greater amount at a specific probability) and *risk permissiveness* for *negative* situations (*e.g.* prefer the possibility but not certainty of losing a certain amount *v.* a guaranteed lesser amount). Thus, the way a decision is constructed is relevant in considerations of risk, uncertainty, and decision making, and technical executives would be well-advised to consider the structure of risk and uncertainty when evaluating alternatives.

Indeed, bearing risk and especially uncertainty is in the realm of managers and entrepreneurs. The generation of profitability, in a larger sense, then ties to some assessment of risk and uncertainty, and understanding the unpredictability of human activity, which can (and does) even dominate over risk probabilities. Those willing to accept risk/uncertainty in decision making have been found to be more independent, progressive, and have a willingness of making decisions with "imperfect" information. While virtually all managing professionals will tend to collect more information, attempt to view the decision and data differently, as well as try to "manage" (as much as possible) the decision (*e.g.* look for examples by others; attempt to change the decision; break the decision down into smaller parts, *etc.*), the most effective executives can embrace ambiguity, and make a decision with potentially unclear circumstances, maximizing mitigation of both risk and uncertainty.

Hence, Avi's need for certainty was based on both his engineering background and personality, manifest in his hobby of aviation. He clearly needed to have a level of certainty behind his support for the product development team, which while potentially understood by technical colleagues, was considered a delay from the other parts of the team, including his commercial teammates. While the level of information needed for comfort on decisions is different for different individuals, the ability to create value is related to the ability to manage risk and uncertainty as much as possible, based on imperfect information. While it can be preferable in a controlled experiment to wait until all of the data has been analyzed, regretfully in the commercial or development *milieu* it is rare for a situation to occur where virtually all ambiguity is removed. Hence, it is the job of the technical executive to make decisions in situations where perhaps on an R&D basis it is "too early" or there is a "lack of information" – although there is some information – because otherwise it will most likely be either too late or the situation will have changed, often to become even more ambiguous. Hence, technical executives need to understand the risk probabilities, and define the uncertainty, applying experience and garnering input to come to prompt decisions, after analyzing the situation with problem-defining skills of a technical professional. While this is not to suggest *rash* decisions should be the norm, it does suggest letting circumstances make a decision is often not effecting managerial responsibility.

"He who hesitates is lost".

-Attributed to Cato

RISK, UNCERTAINTY, AND DISRUPTIVE INNOVATION

As has been noted, disruptive innovation refers to the potential for technologies not of the firm or organization to replace even dominant ones within a given marketplace. The very nature of disruptive innovations suggests that there is relatively low risk against the market leader (they typically serve smaller and more niche markets, and do not directly compete). Moreover, the vast majority of products do *not* result in successful replacement of products from the dominant player. Indeed, most innovations are continuous innovations – they do not result in the need of the customer to change behavior; an example of this is the constant improvement of microprocessor chips used in various computers; contrast that to discontinuous innovation, where there *is* a change of behavior necessary, such as the compact disc player compared to the cassette player for listening to music. Often, continuous innovations are from the original manufacturer, and discontinuous innovations emerge from either the original or a new player in the field. Similarly, as defined by Clayton Christensen, *sustaining innovation* is from the company of the original technology (*e.g.* Honey Nut Cheerios from Cheerios) and maintains a market, while *breakout* innovation while increasing the technologic sophistication still does not change the market or require changes in use (such as a netbook computer). There is risk of all of these types of innovation – uptake and/or changes in characteristics effecting different uses, for example; however, for continuous innovations, it could be argued that there is less uncertainty, compared to discontinuous innovations.

As noted, disruptive innovations have the potential to advance within different markets often unimpeded. While having low risk to the market leader (based on probabilities of new products being successful in the marketplace in general, and taking over a dominant position in specific), they tend to have high uncertainty, given how disruptive innovations can advance unexpectedly, and the ability to take over progressively larger markets (low-end market disruption) (see Figure 6.1).

In this case, the dominant player does not have a crystal ball, and thus cannot predict which technology will result in a threat for the future. However, the technical executive has a skill set that allows for at least the identification of

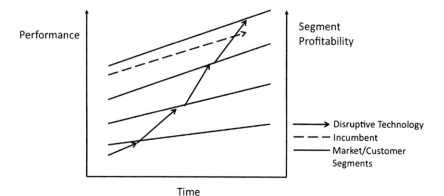

FIGURE 6.1   Low-end market disruption. A technology can enter into a low profitability market/customer segment; subsequent innovation allows movement to progressively higher value segments, eventually displacing the market leader. Adapted from Liang BC, *The Pragmatic MBA for Scientific and Technical Executives*, New York: Academic Press, 2013.

TABLE 6.2 Adopter Segments

Innovators	First 2.5% of adopters; tend to be younger, more educated and more financially secure
Early Adopters	Next 13.5% of adopters; buy during growth phase and more integrated into communities; "Opinion Leaders"
Early Majority	34% of adopters; of average socioeconomic status, with more risk aversion; wait for product acceptance before committing to purchase during late growth phase
Late Majority	34% of adopters; a conservative group with less education and socioeconomic status, who will only adopt a product because of economic or social reasons when products have reached maturity
Laggards	16% of adopters; only adopt a product at the end of the life cycle with active resistance to change; lowest socioeconomic status

possible disrupters of the market, and thus plays a valuable role in detection of these for the organization. Importantly, the technical executive also plays a key strategic role in increasing the *risk* for the potential disrupters, by helping create life cycle improvements, absconding (legally!) with and integration of key traits of other marketed products into the organizational product offerings, and pushing technologic standards that favor the market leader. These interventions make the progression of the potential disruptive technology more difficult (and at times impossible) given the restrictions it places on the disrupter companies and products. In contrast, those technical executives involved in disruptive organizations need to ensure their respective products have firmly established a beachhead in the marketplace in order to use current customers as reference to the next customer segment (as described by Moore, see References). In this way, progressive adoption with gradual product innovation from the disrupter company will be able to meet the needs of the ensuing adopter segment, thus "crossing the chasm" from early adopters to the more profitable early majority (see Table 6.2 for Adopter Segments). Progressive adoption to the disruptive technology will increase the risk (and potentially the uncertainty) for dominant firms in the marketplace, by potentially moving toward higher value market/customer segments.

RISK, UNCERTAINTY, AND DOMINANT DESIGN

As part of the development of products, there are significant levels of technological discontinuities, manifest as both risk and uncertainty. During these times, competition is ongoing in the marketplace to establish a *dominant design*, *viz.* a standard that establishes dominance in a given product category. One of the largest challenges to the technical executive is to recognize the complexity

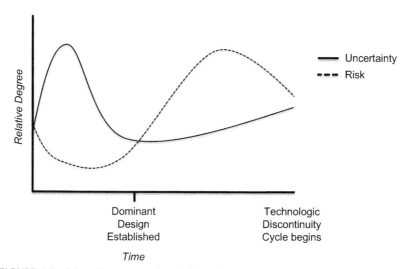

FIGURE 6.2   Schematic representation of risk and uncertainty in a classic model of dominant design cycle. Uncertainty is highest right before a dominant design is established; as the standard becomes clear, uncertainty decreases, and process innovation begins, associated with increased risk with better understood probabilities.

of factors influencing the emergence of a dominant design, and attempt to mitigate the circumstances around it in favor of the organization. It is here, however, where decisions can be quite difficult, as (1) the dominant design can take a significant time to become apparent (*e.g.* years, and sometimes never, such as in the Wii/Playstation/Xbox consoles) and (2) that the technological superiority of a product is *not* the driver of the dominant design (although it can play a significant role). Indeed, like other influences on the business, dominant design can also have influence from cultural, competitive, government, and other stakeholders associated with the product. This is a classic area where uncertainty is very visible, and decisions need to be made with limited information on whether there will or will not be an influence on the evolving current standard. In addition, in the more traditional sense, subsequent to the emergence of a dominant design which suggests stabilization of the product within the marketplace, a process innovation cycle begins, which provides incremental improvements of the dominant design, and focuses on cost reductions and economy of scale. These components of the dominant design cycle have defined *risk* associated with them, having empiric attributes that can be addressed with an understanding of the development value chain. While uncertainty still exists, decisions encompassing risk reduction will allow for efficiencies to be obtained, which include less uncertainty than with the establishment of product dominant design (Figure 6.2). Hence, both risk and uncertainty are clearly impactful on the dominant design cycle, and provide the technical executive a challenge in influencing a dominant design as well as the associated process innovations after emergence. Additional complexity occurs when both the dominant design and the process innovations occur simultaneously, which creates the need to be especially cognizant of the bilateral influences of risk and uncertainty on each other when developing approaches to product *and* process.

USING SKUNK WORKS TO MITIGATE RISK AND UNCERTAINTY

The term skunk works was ostensibly coined at Lockheed, and defined a project that was under wraps and otherwise autonomous and isolated from the general organization. Today, skunk works often refers to a project or program not falling into the hierarchy of the organization and is otherwise independent, and may or may not have support of senior management. As a mechanism to produce products and/or services, there are schools of thought suggesting that this is an important way to generate innovation within a larger firm. Parenthetically, however, there are those who note that this concept may be undesirable in the whole, given the failure rate of these expeditions. If a department requires much of its overall resources for maintaining day-to-day operations, or if there is a requirement that the opportunity developed by the skunk works must be brought back and integrated into the systems of the larger firm, then a skunk works may not be realistic. Since it does indeed require significant resources to maintain a skunk works, and these live best as independent units, the level of commitment must be understood in order to journey down this pathway. Uncertainty is invariably high within these efforts, as most are driven by experimentation and at times numerous failures.

Regardless, if it is assumed that skunk works can drive a level of innovative thought, then a potential value of these units is to mitigate both risk and uncertainty within the organization around technical incrementalism, *viz.* the failures of success. Small, innovative technology companies work essentially as skunk works, experimenting and pushing limits with more emphasis on determining what might work, than why approaches may not; they tend to be optimistic in outcome as well as passionate in execution. As success (if it arrives) emerges, processes must necessarily evolve to create support for the success, and this tends to drive a managerial mindset often more conservative and focused on those activities required to support the business. Hence, while product success uncertainty is high in the early stages of the fledgling company, along with risk, the motivated team continues to work toward product development; with the commencement of adoption, uncertainty of success diminishes (and process innovation risk increases; see above). However, other uncertainty rises; with product success in the marketplace and achieving further adoption and entering into the maturation stage of the product life cycle, there is an increase in uncertainty based on disruptive innovation from others due to internal focus on *sustaining* innovation, *i.e.* technological incrementalism. While these sustaining innovations are very important to managing the life cycle of the product, the technical executive needs to consider potential disrupting technologies and ways (as noted) to stave off these other potential competitive threats early, addressing both uncertainty and risk. Skunk works or other like-minded mechanisms can be part of this approach; creating an organization with the capability to support commercialized products as well as innovate has been associated with ongoing success of firms – this has been referred to as the "ambidextrous" organization. The ambidextrous approach thus includes not only the organizational "system" inherent in product support and life cycle management, but also the creation of radical substitutes, often through a separate and autonomous team whose purpose is to innovate new approaches. This tactic helps mitigate some of the uncertainty of potential disruptive innovation, as well as the risk of a mature product in the marketplace; indeed, the ability to cannibalize one's *own* products (and processes) in the marketplace has been found to be highly correlated to competitive advantage. As the technical executive evaluates the portfolio of assets, in addition to managing internal innovation, creating opportunities for both sustaining and radical innovation as well as monitoring for disruptive innovation are tantamount activities.

"Don't look back. Someone might be gaining on you".

-Leroy "Satchel" Paige

Internal Disruption: The Skunk works of EBOs (Emerging Business Opportunities)

The Emerging Business Opportunities concept originated from the understanding by the then Chairman and CEO of IBM, Lou Gerstner, Jr. that many promising new areas had been either cut or had significant reductions by cost cutting in order to respond to quarterly needs, despite being promising in opportunity. While IBM had many creative new ideas, filing thousands of patents on a yearly basis, the company's systems often had significant difficulty moving from idea to businesses; this included IBM concepts such as the relational database as well as the router, which were successfully commercialized by Oracle and Cisco. In response, the strategic group within the company began identifying promising ideas, and instead of assigning junior executives within business units to address these, assigned them to experienced executives, either alone or perhaps with one colleague, to start a new business. These executives require transition time from running established businesses, where control and knowledge of the business is expected, to being in a new environment where there are many unknowns and experiments and learnings need to occur regularly. As well, this was within the context of minimal resources, especially human resources; increasing FTEs (full-time equivalents) when still in a discovery phase, while potentially required in established businesses, is unwise in these environments. With IBM, however, despite limited resources provided, the EBOs have access to the vast experience and databases within the company; this can help the EBO heads create market experiments that can inform on whether a market exists, can be developed, and/or can be exploited in new ways. The EBOs target is to build businesses collectively that can contribute 2%/year to the company's growth – about US$2B of new revenue, with each individual EBO having

Continued

Internal Disruption: The Skunk works of EBOs (Emerging Business Opportunities)—cont'd

between 5 and 7 years to grow a profitable business. This program has been both a cultural and financial success; from 2000 to 2005, 25 new EBOs were begun, with 3 being shut down; the remaining 22 were generating US$15B in revenue, which at the time was growing at 40% per year. Senior executives began not only to provide information and advice to EBOs, but began to seek out both learnings from these units, and requesting opportunities to head one. By creating internal opportunities for innovation, IBM was able to take advantage of its significant resources by minimizing them, creating skunk works, headed by talented executives allowing creativity to flourish, and disruptive innovations to be developed by the company.
Deutschman A. Building a Better Skunk Works. Fast Company, March 1, 2005.

A FINAL WORD ABOUT CORPORATE STRATEGY, RISK, AND UNCERTAINTY

Corporate strategy is tied integrally with both risk and uncertainty. As noted, the strategy of the firm as expressed is manifest by the adoption of sub-strategies and tactics, translating the corporate to the divisional and below. As technical executives, who contribute to the corporate strategy and define the conversion to the areas of the company within our remit, the understanding of risk and uncertainty cannot be underestimated when thinking about strategy. Because these articulations of strategy will guide decision making in all areas of the organization, it is important *a priori* to ensure that these strategies can indeed encompass potential risks and uncertainties that may arise during the day-to-day interfaces internal throughout the firm and in considerations to the external environment. Impotent strategies that are either too limited, or merely tactical in origin, will exacerbate the uncertainties and worsen the risks under which the organization must operate. Having a firm understanding of what risks and uncertainties reflect both internally and externally, and a granular comprehension of the customer and market segments, can significantly aid in the construction of a corporate strategy that is generally applicable to the organization. Corporate strategies and translated technical ones that guide members of the organization clearly can create value, as long as they are comprehensive and thoughtful enough to address risks and uncertainties.

REFERENCES

Christensen, C.M., 1997. The Innovator's Dilemma: When New Technologies Cause Great Firms to Fail. Harvard Business Press, Boston.

Fleming, L., 2001. Recombinant Uncertainty in Technological Search. Management Science 47, 117–132.

Moore, G.A., 1991. Crossing the Chasm. HarperBusiness Books, New York.

Tushman, M.L., O'Reilly, C.A., 2002. Winning through Innovation: A Practical Guide to Heading Organizational Change and Renewal. Harvard University Press, Boston.

Decision Making is Hard

"The risk of a wrong decision is preferable to the terror of indecision".

-Maimonides

"Whenever you see a successful business, someone once made a courageous decision"

-Peter F. Drucker

"I am enthusiastic over humanity's extraordinary and sometimes very timely ingenuities. If you are in a shipwreck and all the boats are gone, a piano top buoyant enough to keep you afloat may come along and make a fortuitous life preserver. This is not to say, though, that the best way to design a life preserver is in the form of a piano top. I think we are clinging to a great many piano tops in accepting yesterday's fortuitous contrivings as constituting the only means for solving a given problem".

-R. Buckminster Fuller

Andy, the Analyst Andy was an excellent scientist, with an impressive knowledge base as well as analytical mindset. He had worked in a couple of different companies at the department level in manufacturing, and had been responsible for a myriad of different program units. While part of the manufacturing operations division, he was often sought out to brainstorm on issues affecting the value chain in the research group as well as other manufacturing areas; he was excellent at identifying inconsistencies and problems which may not have been initially apparent. After a decade in the division, though, he sought a transfer out, into the commercial area. This both surprised and challenged his then supervisors, since they had been unaware of Andy's interest outside of the technical side of the organization. Even more surprisingly, despite working on a multitude of teams and cross-organizational efforts, the commercial groups (marketing, sales, market research, and corporate development) all demurred when asked about a transfer into their respective units. Indeed, the only potential opportunity into which the

Managing and Leading for Science Professionals. http://dx.doi.org/10.1016/B978-0-12-416686-8.00007-4
67

commercial group was willing to put Andy was the product support group, at a relatively entry level position, despite his previous experience. As a favor to Andy, the global head of manufacturing discussed this with one of his colleagues in the market research group; Andy was obviously good at identifying issues, and the technical part of the organization had valued him both in research and manufacturing. How could they not want someone with obvious analytical and on-the-ground experience as Andy represented?

IDENTIFICATION OF A PROBLEM ISN'T ENOUGH

Decisions within organizations are based on a number of factors, as noted, within not only the context of the culture of the company, but the risk and uncertainties that exist; moreover, the relative level of ambiguity can be high and is clearly something that can at times cause "paralysis" due to the perceived need to completely scrutinize the situation ("analysis"; hence, "paralysis by analysis"). This occurs at all parts of the organization, certainly, and is something often cited both culturally having developed with organizational maturation, as well as part of a pejorative notation in the growth of companies. However, as mentioned earlier, the ability to hone in on issues and determine where the particular weaknesses lie is a key skill of the technical executive; our analytical abilities are focused on finding the "soft spots" in order to shore up our data sets and in particular justify any conclusions that we might make based on the data. A cautionary note has already been sounded regarding having to wait for all the data to be apparent before making decisions (see Chapter 6), but notwithstanding, it is clear that being able to pick out the infirmities of challenging situations where decisions need be made is an important skill.

With that in mind, one of the specific areas where many technical executives need experience is the *next* step after issue identification, *viz.* solution generation. Andy had been noted to have a robust level of analytical ability, and was helpful in brainstorming sessions for his colleagues; however, his lack of acceptance into the commercial groups suggested that he had difficulty emerging from just pinpointing problems to generating solutions. While as noted it is relevant to identify potential concerns (and frequently expected of technical executives), not being able to provide alternatives creates a myriad of problems, from motivational issues to the perception of not being a positive contributor in the context of a solution-based team. There are a number of studies on team management noting the need for idea generation at various levels (including departmental, multifunctional, and executive); these studies suggest that putting forth issues alone, without potential solutions, creates negativity and discord, which is at best counterproductive. Indeed, as opposed to moving a program forward, such attitudes actually set back the work of the team. The tangible need for facts is undisputable, but the presentation within teams, review groups, and/or executive sessions requires the discipline to not only express issues, but to have thought through these well enough to be able to offer a modicum of solutions. Minimally, that is a responsibility of the managerial leadership of the organization, including technical executives. It is always easier to point out a problem than to construct a solution, and the ability to facilitate both is key for highly functioning firms.

APPROACHES TO SOLUTION GENERATION

There are a myriad of ways to structure at least a thought process around the development of solution(s) to complex organizational problems. Many approaches have been developed that encompass psychological, cultural, and learning theories around patterns of thought that might be helpful (e.g. see sidebar, System Dynamics, Chapter 2). One way that has been used by a variety of R&D groups as well as other firms revolves around a thought process of *initial generation of alternatives*. This is an activity which can be done both in an individual as well as a group setting, but has as its main component the rigor of creating multiple possibilities without necessarily assigning initial potential or judgment around each. The key is to define possible solutions that can act as cognitive anchors by which the situation can be oriented – again, this is a discipline of ensuring that one does not stop at identifying the problem only, and instead creates a framework around which the next step is always considered.

After the generation of alternatives, a refinement of the choices can be made *identifying assumptions* for each. Because most analyses are related to uncertainties and risks, assumptions will need to be made for each of the alternatives, based on the almost certainty that not all of the required information is accessible for the problem at hand. While individuals may object to some of the alternatives, as long as the assumptions are clearly articulated, at a minimum the context and outline of each can well be understood. Indeed, it is difficult to object to any alternative *per se* if the assumptions are laid out logically, and the conversation can shift to considerations of all the alternatives rather than a single one. Parenthetically, oftentimes there is a tendency to "jump" to the "obvious" decision, before creating alternatives – whether as an individual or a group doing such evaluations, there should be some caution in doing this, since there is a level of depth associated with the rigor of considering other potential solutions. Indeed, this can inform the decision even better if others are considered and dismissed.

Finally, after generating alternatives, and identifying the assumptions for potential solutions, the technical executive should articulate the strengths and weaknesses ("pros and cons") of each alternative, and be able to recommend a solution based on the solution generation process. It is interesting to note that cognitively we may unconsciously effect this process in some manner or form, resulting in the "obvious" solution that sometimes becomes apparent. However, by being very conscious about the generation of solution possibilities to our colleagues the thought process is better understood by the entire team, and the rationale for suggesting a solution better accepted as a viable alternative

TABLE 7.1 A Paradigm for Potential Solution Generation

Generate alternatives	Create different possibilities based on the data in hand; suspend judgments on potential until later on in the process
Identify assumptions for each alternative	Clarify the framework around which each alternative should be considered; wrap each alternative around a set of beliefs which are clearly articulated
List the strengths and weaknesses of each alternative	Using the facts available, the data accumulated and the assumptions around each, articulate the strengths and weaknesses of solutions being generated
Suggest a solution	Within the context of the alternatives, assumptions, facts and perceptions, recommend solution(s) to the problem; potentially iterate with an understanding of new facts brought to the table by others

(although perhaps not necessarily the solution to be used, but having impact nonetheless). The relevant factor is that problems alone are not identified without a considered potential for solutions, and the exercise of understanding the assumptions being made can be helpful in the entire team participating in solution creation. Hence, while an individual can utilize this approach, it allows for other members of the group to understand better the rationale for any suggested solution; as a group, this can be used to refine assumptions to accept or reject potential solutions with a more broad level of understanding. Table 7.1 summarizes this approach.

"For every problem, there is a solution that is simple, neat, and wrong".

-H.L. Mencken

THINKING ABOUT THINKING

One of the most interesting things about an organization is the true difference existing between the technical function and the rest of the firm. While the function of the commercial and/or manufacturing part of the organization is really to homogenize (albeit in a granular manner) outputs, whether they be the branding or promotion or distribution or minimization of variance of a product, the R&D function is quite different. In that part of the organization, despite our experiments and prototypes and data generation capabilities, our efforts result in a different output – to generate knowledge, with such knowledge being *heterogeneous*, *viz.* to create concepts and ideas which are *different* and not replicate that which already exists – *i.e.* this knowledge is used to innovate, creating something new. As a result, while the technical executive is tasked with similar responsibilities on a corporate scale as others within the organization, the outputs expected require a different type of mindset for decision making and communication than perhaps those of the other parts of the firm.

As a result, the technical executive is tasked with the responsibility of both understanding the processes of other parts of the organization, where consistency of outputs (reflecting objectives thereof) are relevant, which is in contrast to R&D, where the opposite is required, *viz.* heterogeneous innovative solutions. Measures of productivity are thus, not surprisingly, inconsistent with other parts of the organization, since creativity resulting in commercial success may have a very different time horizon than manufacturing or sales. Factor growth (accumulation of various resources, including people) cannot be counted on to increase performance, as the number of ideas produced does not necessarily correlate to the number of people in the lab. Hence, our decision-making processes – which include budgets, forecasts, capital expenditures *etc.*, while similar to other parts of the organization, do not portend very well to the very essence of the technical part of the firm. Nonetheless, technical professionals must exist within the rubric of the rest of the company, and as a result, need to be able to make decisions within their own functional areas that allow the nature of the R&D function to exist, if not flourish. This involves not only ensuring teams and groups are provided clear guidance and objectives, but that the technical manager is prepared to facilitate the mechanisms that allow for both clear "deliberations" (see below), which translate to good decisions (see also Chapter 12).

As a young technical executive who had spent much time as an individual contributor both within industry and academia, the concept of deliberations was not something with which I was familiar. We as scientists generated data, that data was inspected, and we made *decisions* based on this data for the next steps, be that the ensuing experiment, applying for funding, obtaining resources, or forecasting for the next year. Unconsciously, as noted by Pava (see References) once decisions are ready to be made, the generation of knowledge is essentially completed; the implication is that focus *per se* on decision making conceptually is a framework issue (see Chapter 6), and thus already reflects the biases of the framers. While this can at some level be mitigated by going through a structured process (*e.g.* Table 7.1), an area which the technical professional can also consider is the intervention *at* the aforementioned deliberations. These deliberations are essentially pre-decisions, *while* the knowledge is being generated; it is the process of creating, disseminating, and articulating the data, prior to any decisions around the data being made. It is the work being done as we *formulate* and *come to conclusions about* the data. These activities are often unconscious, or not identified as part of the decision-making process, which is much more mature. The ability to concretize deliberations, specifically, to *make explicit* cognitive processes of data consideration, creates data sets of high quality, allowing the knowledge derived to be reflected in the decisions thereof. This is key for us as technical executives who manage innovation and must make decisions based on these outputs; decisions must have a fundamental base in deliberations in order to be robust.

There are some key processes that can be important for effective deliberation to be helpful for the technical executive (see Passmore in References for a detailed discussion). This reflects not only processes but people, with the attempt to blur the lines between any functional or political areas, but rather to ensure that the knowledge being generated or developed is considered by those appropriate for the area. It is important that those who are intimately familiar with a project or program with the requisite data and knowledge are directly participatory in the deliberation process, rather than only senior representatives of particular teams or departments who, while familiar with the outputs, do not know the details of the data which may have significance. This is not to negate the importance of more senior management; part of the deliberation process must have context around clearly articulated goals as well as timeframes by which deliberations stop and decisions must be made (notwithstanding championing subsequent decisions made). Indeed, what this suggests is that the data set and knowledge being generated must be of high quality to be able to be discussed by the various levels of the team, including senior managers. Removal of biases, including departmental, political, and/or personal (including those disruptive to the process), is imperative to provide the best information for decision making. It is the role of the technical and other executives to ensure that these latter issues do not get in the way of the deliberation, and that the appropriate individuals are in the room to provide relevant input and data. This needs to be performed in a streamlined structure that does not inhibit discussion and motivation – organizational structure within the function, thus, should avoid hierarchy, allow those with the most knowledge to participate in decision making, and be highly integrated where the people who have the most knowledge can work directly with those who need the information, rather than traversing through a potentially filtering bureaucratic system. Part and parcel of this is the ability to widely disseminate information; knowledge should not be only shared with senior managers who then assign it to the teams. Indeed, this is both demotivating and counterproductive – I can recall an example where the relatively new head of R&D at one large biopharmaceutical firm once only allowed the team head, and no other scientists from either the team presenting or other teams, at monthly management meetings (previously welcomed when the company was smaller), since "team leaders should know what's going on with the project, and we tell the teams [through the leaders] what's important". Over the ensuing year productivity within both the discovery and development teams declined, to the point where the CEO brought together the team leaders – without the head of R&D present – to "understand issues"; it was clear that the defined movement of knowledge to those least knowledgeable and decisions being made without requisite input was a key factor in the diminished productivity, notwithstanding a lack of understanding of the rationale of decisions. While the organization in the past had encouraged and shared learnings, removing this opportunity for the scientists and others on teams only served to question members' respective roles in the organization. Table 7.2 summarizes some factors important in the deliberation process.

TABLE 7.2 Factors Important in Deliberations

Familiarity with the data/ knowledge	People with the most detailed knowledge must participate in deliberations
Goals and timelines need to be clear, including process transitioning from deliberation to decision making	Both team members and senior managers must have clarity in these areas
Removal of biases, political undertones, and those disruptive to the process	Senior executives must take responsibility to ensure deliberations move forward consciously without these as issues
Organizational structure appropriate	Sharing of knowledge from those who have the most detailed knowledge to those who require it should be facilitated by use of both team structures (e.g. matrix) as well as avoidance of hierarchies and bureaucratic structures
Avoidance of filtration	Knowledge should as much as possible be transferred from those who know to those who need it – moving through departmental or other structures to senior managers and then back down to teams should be avoided
Learning should be encouraged	For productivity and motivation, creating learning environments which are broadly applicable can not only effect higher productivity, but also moments of epiphany which otherwise would not have been available

DEALING WITH THE INEVITABLE: CONFLICT IN DECISION MAKING

Conflict is a regular part of management, and is in particular a part of decision making. While dealing with differences in opinion in the technical realm can often be adjudicated by the evaluation of data at hand, often decisions that are managerial in nature are less than clear cut. As such, these decisions need to be made based on experience, the weighing of input of others, and usually speed, as noted earlier. The challenge is that such differences between team members, executives, and/or departments can prolong the process of decision making, particularly if those who disagree have particularly influential positions. While conflict can result in better decision-making processes, and that high-quality decisions to a certain extent require conflict, the technical professional needs to be aware that *managing* conflict is the responsibility of executives to ensure motivation is not killed due to the conflict. There is a need to acknowledge that conflict is inevitable, but polarization of positions is not if handled correctly.

Consensus is often noted by many as part of the conflict resolution pathway; it is the approach that many of us take to address an issue. Indeed, once communication, consideration of deliberations, and assumptions are understood by all, conflicts may diminish and new and/or better alternatives may emerge around which all can agree. Certainly, this is a usual process in many well-functioning organizations. However, particularly in complex business decisions, consensus may be ephemeral. Legitimate differences in opinion may exist in situations having never been encountered or are so unique that approaches tried in the past may not apply. Obviously, getting the right people in the room who have deliberated on the issue and have requisite knowledge is important, as well as garnering the experience of others on the situation. Within this, if consensus still cannot be attained, after all stakeholders express their respective opinions, then the most relevant manager – be that the technical executive or delegate – needs to make a decision. While not everyone may agree with the decision, everyone should have had their respective opinion heard, and the technical executive needs to ensure this is the case. Indeed, studies have shown that prompt decisions are key in highly functioning firms, and that while a specific executive's perspective may not be the one ultimately chosen to act upon, the ability to express thoughts and concerns, despite perhaps not ruling the day, still provides influence to and participation in the decision (see Eisenhardt, References). This thus allows conflict to occur, but also allows decision making to be prompt, and participation within the decision.

Organizations must be wary not to be paralyzed by conflict by attempting to construct compromises that maximally satisfy all stakeholders. First, it may be difficult at best to come up with such a solution, and second, it may take an inordinate amount of time to accomplish. Highly functioning organizations avoid being forced into decisions by either self-imposed or arbitrary deadlines; time to decisions often will stretch out to encompass such deadlines and create a limited effort to achieve consensus until the time when a decision needs to be made, and result in an emergent decision where stakeholders may not feel they were able to adequately contribute to the iteration being considered. In fact, as noted, rapid decisions have the advantage of prompting input right away, rather than letting situations change and evolve and create opportunities for competing organizations. We as managers and executives require input, but must realize that uncertainty most likely will not be reduced in the timeframe where a decision must be made. Hence, we will need to make decisions with the knowledge we have, and with the teams that will be impacted by any decisions being made. By integrating these decisions with others that are related, and seeking out the appropriate knowledge (*via* the most knowledgeable people and information to date), as well as understanding the assumptions, one can be confident that all the relevant facts and opinions have been ascertained prior to the decision being made.

"The greatest accomplishment began as a decision once made and often a difficult one".

-Michael Rawls

REFERENCES

Eisenhardt, K.M., 1990. Speed and Strategic Choice: How Managers Accelerate Decision Making. California Management Review 32, 39–54.

Katzenbach, J.R., Smith, D.K., 1993. The Discipline of Teams. Harvard Business Review 17, 111–120.

Passmore, W., 1994. Creating Strategic Change: Designing the Flexible, High Performance Organization. Wiley and Sons, New York.

Pava, C., 1983. Managing New Office Technology: An Organizational Strategy. The Free Press, New York.

Moving Up the Ladder: Abandoning Your Peers?

"If you're not practicing, somebody else is, somewhere, and he'll be ready to take your job".

-Brooks Robinson

"I don't ever remember them telling us or teaching us that the only way we could be more successful is if other people were less successful. They never inculcated the belief that somehow, in order for us to climb the ladder, other people have to come down from the ladder".

-Marco Rubio

"…go in the direction your head is pointed in".

-Jung Chang

The Price of Advancement John had worked at two major companies before coming to the firm, with significant success having both an understanding of product technologies and the competition in the global marketplace. He had developed a diversity of skills, and was clearly an expert in the use, upkeep and further development of technology in the lab, from liquid chromatography to cutting edge cloning techniques. He had, as he termed it, "survived" several reorganizations in his previous firm, and in fact increased the group reporting to him, presumably based on his technical abilities. Indeed, he was often asked to be part of various outside seminars and webinars as a result, and worked well with colleagues in different companies. Moreover, he was an avid hockey player, and participated on the company team; in fact, he converted the team from roller hockey to an ice hockey team, arranging for everything from ice time to team schedules. Despite being a goalie, he was considered an anchor of the team, where others depended on him to ensure everything from current scheduling to making sure pucks were available for warm up. After games he was often the last person in the locker room, conversing with each member of the team socially. Subsequent to the second season, John was promoted to a high-level R&D position, where his responsibility encompassed areas within both research and development. His exposure to previous teammates diminished during the workday, and although he still played on the hockey team, he found that conversations were more strained, or more related to the political or "behind the scenes" aspects of company business. He noted that in one instance, two teammates whom he knew quite well, stopped talking when he walked into the locker room, with the silence broken only when John began a conversation. John felt like an outsider. What had happened?

CHANGES IN PERSPECTIVE

While there are times when technical professionals are promoted because of their people skills, or their ability to motivate, the vast majority of times it is a function of their technical skills allowing them to progress up the proverbial ladder in the organization. While the recognition of the position and inherent competence associated with the promotion is gratifying, it changes the perspective of those within the area, particularly if a reporting structure changes. While leadership is about establishing and maintaining relationships, because of both real and perceived power changes, the relationships with those who are lower on the reporting hierarchy will be different. This is manifest by changes in such relationships, with former co-workers (or hockey teammates) viewing the new technical manager differently than before. There might be some that try to take advantage of previous relationships, others who are truly happy of the new success, and even others who are secretly jealous of these changes. The reality is that within the work environment, the challenges for the technical professional (especially the ones related to people) increase because of the positional changes. This is also reflected on how the new technical manager responds – with exposure to at least some of the aforementioned changes from previous peer relationships, executives can become suspicious ("they're only being nice to me because they need something") or cynical ("my playing time is increasing only because I'm a director now"). By understanding that these changes may/will occur, technical executives can acknowledge that within the workplace, friendships can exist but that they will be different with the individuals who were part of their previous network. It is a new responsibility to expand the work network to include those at a peer level as well. This reinforces both the maintenance of current relationships (albeit with an understanding that they will change in nature) as well as developing new ones, which will be important with the increased responsibility derived from the promotion. Indeed, this is part of the responsibility of the technical executive in order to be effective in the new role.

John needed to realize that, in fact, his relationships as much as he wanted them to be the same – being one of the guys on the team – would be different because of the nature of the work environment, reflected even after hours in a place as different as a hockey rink. The fact that teammates would behave differently is a clear manifestation of the changed relationships now existing, despite any real changes in behavior John may have effected. As a technical manager, it would be to John's advantage to understand the perspective of his teammates, and be cognizant of a new relationship being created due to his positional change.

MANAGING WHAT YOU (DON'T) SAY: RESPONSIBILITY IN COMMUNICATION

As noted, with changes in position, there comes a different level of communication from the organization; often this means information comes earlier or more restricted in distribution from higher levels than previously. It is important to understand that the responsibility of the technical executive is to appropriately act on information representative of the position. However, it is particularly important for new executives to be especially careful about offhand remarks, especially in the presence of previous peers. Moreover, for direct reports who may have been peers in the past, careful consideration on communication with deliberate understanding of areas that should not be addressed is key in order to preserve trust and not burden others with information which might be sensitive, notwithstanding the responsibility of confidentiality. Certainly, this may be noted as common sense, particularly given management training that often occurs to prepare new managers for these issues. However, there have been many occasions where peer pressure from those in earlier networks may manifest as being trustworthy; *a good rule of thumb is that everything a manager says to a subordinate is for the public record (and everything said to the manager from the subordinate should never be)*. This is a lesson that has been learned by many new technical (and other) managers, and has large ramifications when dealing with issues such as resource expenditures or human resource issues such as layoffs. As much as trust was part of the relationships with former colleagues and team members, the changes in position require a different level of scrutiny. Indeed, this is again seen both with those who were peers previously as much as the relationships currently existing; as much as there were liabilities perceived to his teammates in the locker room for John to hear the conversation, there were now similar liabilities for John to speak about his day at the office. Managing this transition is key for success for the technical executive.

GRIPE SESSIONS AND GALLOWS HUMOR

In any field there are trials and tribulations inherent in training. As example, as a (former) physician, the rigor of medical school, internship, residency, and fellowship has the reminiscence and similarities of an incarceration experience. The level of information to be assimilated (memorized), the numerous evaluations, the translations into a practical work product, the teams to be part of, and the requisite less than pleasant tasks needed to endure to ensure that all the work gets done, notwithstanding the lack of sleep and time off in a regimented monolithic system are certainly an experience one goes through because one WANTS to do it, or alternatively, because one HAS to do it; indeed, you only get out when your time is done. As noted earlier, graduate school, post-doctoral training, business school *etc.* all have similar points of contrition, but which are endured (for some of us, encompassing multiple journeys) due to our understanding and orientation toward a goal. As a way to carry on these chosen paths, we often resort to coping mechanisms that can be both healthy and disarming, allowing a level of stress relief for all involved. Indeed, as part of a multitude of departments, I was able to view (and participate) first hand in the various defense mechanisms – *e.g.* in medicine, seeing and learning about various types of pathology induced many of us to personify in ourselves and others our experiences with the various diseases, which we were either studying or had been exposed to in our clinical training; on the technical side, comparisons of our thesis advisor's comments to mounds of "stuff" we needed to climb (and sink within) on our Sisyphean task of writing our thesis was not only commonplace but considered by some a creative outlet. Moreover, sessions (formal or otherwise) were also fairly frequent where we would actively and vociferously voice our concerns to our peers (but never to our supervisors). All of these activities were a part of a psychological release and bonding which prevents being consumed by the experience(s); they are coping mechanisms. As a peer associated activity, the gallows humor and the gripe sessions were part of the environment.

Not unexpectedly, these types of activities extend to the organizational *milieu*, where there are indeed stresses reminiscent of times of training or when very junior in an organization. "Joking up" is a frequent pastime in many organizations, where superiors are poked fun at, and "problem sessions" can be an impromptu occurrence where the natural imperfections of those above us (no one is perfect) can be complained about. In a sense, this can reflect a healthy organization that allows both transparency in communication as well as the ability to work in an accepting environment. However, for the technical executive, one must be wary within these areas, since the level of responsibility has changed, as has the perspective from peers and subordinates. Specifically, there is an obligation to the organization that needs to be paramount in consideration when encountering these types of situations. Indeed, while managers are not unaware of many of the issues that may be occurring within the firm, and carry about the same (or more) challenges and concerns and heartache that everyone else does, this position cannot necessarily be articulated. Jumping into the fray of either joking or complaining without careful consideration (if ever) while initially may be considered a way to show empathy or build camaraderie, it does neither – in fact, this challenges the credibility of the technical manager, potentially their superiors, and the rest of the organization. This is particularly true in gripe sessions. These can be very helpful if managed in a way that allows true empathy to be expressed, but challenges the group to go from identification of issues *per se* to one where defined problems are expressed, *as well as alternative solutions* and next steps (*"solution transitioning"*) (see Chapter 7). This will not only create a constructive environment, but also provide an opportunity to learn as well as motivate the group, as a manager and leader who is actively listening and helping provide solutions. It is important for the technical manager to understand that the role no longer involves contributing to those activities that might have been more appropriate when at a more junior level, but to support the organization in allowing for communication, and driving solutions rather than prolonged discontent, which will undermine the goals of the organization. It is clear that this does require an arm's length positioning from these activities, which is a necessary part of both the management and leadership responsibility of the technical executive. A more constructive outlet for the technical manager when encountering issues such as these is to discuss with one's own supervisor, or a mentor (see Chapter 11).

"Analyzing humor is like dissecting a frog. Few people are interested and the frog dies of it".

-EB White

MANAGING DISCONTENT: IS IT ME OR IS IT YOU?

Our collective goal as managers is to maximize the creation of value within our organization. Mechanistically, as much as technical and other executives attempt to create a working environment fostering innovation, satisfaction, and growth to create such value, with employees motivated each day to actively participate in the organization, often we miss the mark. Indeed, in a global study by Deloitte (Talent Edge 2020, see References), only about 35% of employees at large corporations when surveyed in March of 2011 expected to be with their current employer to the end of the year; reasons cited were uncertain career paths, distrust in current leadership, and limitations in keeping top performing employees. This certainly begs the question of whether we as managers are recognizing, understanding, and/or unconsciously fomenting discontent amongst our employees, to the point where the vast majority would be willing to articulate that they do not plan on staying with the organization. As noted, no manager or set of managers is perfect, so there is always the potential for discontent; the key is not only to proactively prevent those actions which could induce such a situation, but also be able to actively recognize the signs in order to address concerns early.

COMMUNICATION AND TRUST

Already noted are the issues around communication and trust. These aspects both support and create motivation when positive (particularly when accompanied by clarity and transparency around expectations and feedback) and destroy such when existing suboptimally. Particularly in the technical environment, which can be dominated by introverted individuals, the communication component has an especially important aspect, since anecdotes suggest that oral or written communication could have occurred, but in fact understanding did not; we as technical executives need to ensure that messages are both delivered and received when we are interacting with subordinates, which (hopefully!) will generate the first step to clarity and thus to trust. Indeed, without a relationship, communication, and trust, we as managers cannot hope to understand the interests and objectives, and thus the motivating factors, of the employees of which we are associated. Hence, our level of communication must engender an understanding from the perspective of the key messages we are delivering, but also active listening to both be clear of any concerns as well as an appreciation that we have been understood.

MICROMANAGEMENT

Another aspect noted earlier that drives discontent is the supervisor's lack of understanding of the appropriate role he or she is to play vis-à-vis the employee. This has been mentioned within issues of control and/or credit; it has also been articulated as *micromanagement*. Of the many ways to demotivate employees (and managers!), micromanagement is probably one of the most effective to generate employee dissatisfaction. Micromanagement is defined as the constant assistance and requirement for an employee to consult with the supervisor before making any decisions, no matter how small. It is an important aspect to be wary for technical as well as other executives, since our abilities as *junior* members of the team revolve around the abilities to accomplish tasks (see Chapter 1). The empowerment of subordinates in the organization is thus part of the concept of trust, and indicates that the decisions and mechanisms for execution of experiments, prototypes, trials, or workups is valued within the organization, and that the employee plays an important part within that context. While every manager must make an assessment at what point it is appropriate to step into either the decision-making process or provide more detailed guidance, it is important to realize that providing the opportunity for the employee to practice making decisions and working through problems (and generating solutions, see Chapter 7) is an important part of their development, and is best for the organization as a whole. Again, this revolves around trust and communication.

"There is excessive micromanagement, with far too many decisions being taken in the Treasury by bright young things who have no feel for the practical problems on the ground".

-Vince Cable

REWARD SYSTEMS

Reward systems also are an important component of the organizational structure that increases contentment within the work *milieu*. Clearly, as technical managers we need to be cognizant that a high level of morale is important in team-like situations. Indeed, while there are some individuals who may prefer to work independently (see Chapter 3, Career Anchors), even such individuals appreciate recognition of their work and the competence they have achieved. Indeed, the reward systems are both monetary and nonmonetary in this context; while bonuses and salary are part of this rubric, the demonstration of a supervisor to an employee both publically and privately of a job well done is an important component of a reward system to harness the most important resource of the firm. Hence, we as technical managers need to appreciate those rewards that maximize value for our team members. In the Deloitte survey mentioned earlier, employee discontentment was found to be significantly related to a lack of either appreciation of the talent within the organization, and the lack of focus on recognition *via* salary or opportunities for advancement within the company. This included not only promotion, but opportunities for training and further skill development. As technical professionals, this is particularly relevant, as the burgeoning of knowledge within our fields, and the need to keep up with all of the new information being generated daily, is a significant responsibility within our respective groups.

MANAGEMENT BEHAVIOR

Finally, we ourselves as supervisors may foment discontent amongst our groups by ignoring the personal interaction needed to show commitment to those we supervise. While this does not imply every employee should be a best friend, it does suggest that, as has been seen by many motivational studies (see Steers, References), many employees become discontented with their current work environment when they *perceive* that management is treating them either poorly or dismissively. An often cited example is the manager who notes that employees are being paid, so "should be happy they have a job", and act accordingly; this clearly does not engender respect to either the manager or the organization in general that would promote someone as such to a management position. This happens all along the employee chain; indeed, I have seen venture capital board members note that companies can "survive" without the current CEO; after the expression of that sentiment, the CEO began looking for another job, and left the company several months later, with two weeks' notice; the company was then sold for a loss a year later due to both a lack of leadership within the company, as well as the hesitant perception of a company where the CEO would leave so abruptly. We as technical executives should be aware that our roles evolve to include an interpersonal skill set to ensure that the organization's policies and strategies are followed while relating to our groups in a personal, non-dehumanizing way.

ORGANIZATIONAL ISSUES AND APPROACHES

In contrast to this, despite the technical executive providing a *milieu* of empowerment, motivation, and opportunity, there are employees who continue to be unhappy. These employees often show both aggressive and passive aggressive tendencies (see Table 8.1), both reducing productivity and creating an atmosphere of doubt within the team or department. It is important to identify these employees and the issue(s) causing their concern as early as possible before their discontentment spreads to others.

Of note is that such employees may not be unhappy due to the organization or the management thereof; there may be personal problems and stresses at home or in the family environment causing the issues. We as technical managers need to ensure that we can probe discreetly in the context of our notation of some of the aspects noted in Table 8.1 in order to determine if these are issues that either require our assistance or intervention. This communication may be a new aspect for the technical executive, where such "personal" questions may be uncomfortable at first; however, for the benefit of the employee and organization we are obligated to ferret out the root causes of such issues and address them. Assistance from our own managers and human resource managers may be of significant value when encountering such issues, both in detection as well as providing potential options for solution.

Notwithstanding personal issues, understanding organizational issues creating discontent of employees is tantamount. For technical professionals, it has been noted that working on challenging and important projects within the company as well as being cited for technical competence of solving difficult

TABLE 8.1 Employee Tendencies Suggesting Discontent

Avoiding meetings

Not completing work on time, especially if done so previously

Diminished work quality, especially if high quality previously

Avoiding responsibility

Being disruptive

Absenteeism

Outright disobedience

problems (and recognition inside and outside the company) are particularly relevant factors in creating employee satisfaction. These are important to real ize on the technical side of the organization, but should be understood on a broader level, especially when the technical executive begins managing those outside of R&D specifically. Indeed, as noted previously, a lack of clarity on career pathways and inadequate training (either in leadership development or technically) creates a *milieu* of discontent that pushes staff to look elsewhere for opportunities. If there is lack of clarity on the strategy of the company, or a lack of understanding where the employee fits into that strategy, this generates a lack of trust in the organizational leadership, which also creates discontent. These may all occur outside the manager–subordinate relationship, based on the organizational structure that currently exists. We as technical managers need to be wary of these organizational sources of discontent even as we address our day-to-day interactions with employees.

There are, however, those employees who are discontent, not due to personal or organizational reasons, but because of issues they are reticent to reveal, and thus are very difficult to manage. Such employees manifest in a variety of phenotypes – *e.g.* those who avoid work regularly, argue consistently with superiors at every opportunity, will not work with others, and/or manifest every change as a dramatic event. Of note is that such behavior is consistent; this is not the occasional outburst or pushback, but one which is pathologically manifest on an unfailing basis *and results in decreased productivity* by either direct or indirect (*e.g.* team) effects. There are often deep-seated reasons for the behavior of these employees, and while it should be the first consideration of the man- ager to attempt to ascertain the cause (see above) in many cases this is just not possible. Regardless, it is important to address these types of behaviors early, but note it is best to do so after personally performing a careful evaluation of the situation – this includes obtaining all the relevant facts (*cf.* hearsay) of the situation, attempting to triangulate on the behavior from a variety of different sources. Once the facts are understood, and there still appears to be an issue, it is important to plan an intervention, which may include others (*e.g.* human resources). Such actions should be a formal and individualized meeting, where behavior is identified in a calm and unthreatening manner, especially noting the impact on the team, and addressing the behavior rather than the person. While the staff member may interrupt and deny such behavior, elaboration on the personal fact finding and specific examples should be used judiciously at this juncture to articulate the point. It is obviously important in a respectful manner to have a dialogue about the issue, and certainly allow the employee to provide his/her perspective; however, the key is to be able to develop a solution to the issue at hand, which is appropriate and acceptable to all parties. Here again, active listening is important (Chapter 5), which might provide some clue as to why the behavior might be manifest. It may take several meetings to ensure that the problematic behaviors are corrected; as technical executives, seeing continu- ous improvement is important, as overnight shifts in behavior are at best dif- ficult. By agreeing to a solution the ownership of the issue becomes mutual and

TABLE 8.2 Approach to Deal with Problematic Behavior in Employees

Ascertain potential causes	Evaluate background and history of employee in the company (and previous companies, if available) noting confidentiality at all times
Gather the facts	Personally look into the situation and speak with directly and indirectly involved individuals; observe behavior if possible
Create a plan for action	Determine an appropriate meeting time and requisite involvement from other groups as necessary (e.g. human resources)
Act promptly	Meet with the employee and identify the issue, focusing on how it impacts the team and productivity, avoiding personalizing the issue to the individual
Create solutions	Advise and assist the employee as much as possible to create and buy into a mutually acceptable solution
Monitor	Continue to monitor the issue providing appropriate positive or negative feedback

allows both the manager and the employee to move ahead together, on the same team. However, it is important that if the etiology of the issue is due to issues that are beyond the expertise of the technical professional (*e.g.* health issues), that the employee be referred to the appropriate services within the company (often human resources) to address. Moreover, if despite the communication, articulated understanding, and agreement (or lack thereof) there are continued issues with behavior, these will need to be documented and acting to change the position of the employee to one where they might be more successful (if available) or termination (if not) should be instituted. Table 8.2 summarizes this approach.

A FINAL WORD: MANAGING YOUR FORMER PEERS

Some of this has already been discussed in various situations above, but it is important to point out that when accepting a role requiring a change in relationship between former peers and direct responsibility for the activities of the group, there are certain tendencies of both the manager and the team that can occur. While the temptation is initially to approach and evaluate the former peer–new manager relationship, often a more sanguine approach is to seek advice and clarity from one's new manager. The rationale behind this is to ensure that the expectations for not only the technical executive are clear, but that of the entire group; this is especially important if this is the first experience managing others. By having a firm understanding of the expectations of more senior management, the technical executive can have a clear and line-of-sight approach when subsequently communicating with new reports on the goals, strategy and tactics of the organization in the context of the group. With communication to the group, this enhances the credibility of the technical executive to both more senior managers and to the team as a whole. Indeed, the communication with the team subsequent to this meeting with one's own supervisor is a paramount activity to demonstrate leadership, by understanding the expectations of the organization of the group, and within the team to provide precise and clear guidance. As a first step, this provides a level of trust and communication that hopefully engenders a firm and positive starting point between the manager and new reports.

During the initial sets of communications with former peers, it may be at times uncomfortable to demonstrate levels of authority due to previous relationships. While this may be due to being in a new position *per se*, often it is the conscious or unconscious fear of losing friendships and camaraderie both in the present or engendered in the past. I have seen even experienced managers fail to retain some of their objectiveness when dealing with former peers, particularly in human resource issues like conflict resolution, or when promotions and layoff decisions need to be made. It is certainly understandable that we tend to take into account our previous associations when making decisions; however, we need to ensure that by doing so we do not create either true or perceived biases, and lose respect by appearing to favor our former co-workers. One way to potentially avoid this is to not only scrutinize our decisions, but ensure that we communicate and align expectations with all of the team, both in a group setting, such as a staff or group meeting, as well as individually, on regular one-on-one meetings. Both of these forums are necessary to ensure that we obtain feedback in a variety of settings, and that we are publically accountable for decisions being made. Moreover, it allows both the group, and in particular, individual members the opportunity to understand our perspectives, both managerially and programmatically, and to ensure alignment is taking place. Indeed, this is especially true if the group is somewhat large and one's previous association was only with a limited number of the group.

A specific caution is to avoid dramatic action within the first few weeks of becoming a supervisor to former peers. Because one was previously a member of the group, it may seem that we may know of all the issues and problems that need to be repaired, or processes that require intervention based on our experience alone. Notwithstanding having new subordinates becoming acquainted with a new leadership style, having to alter programs, processes, and/or infrastructure can be demanding to even the most experienced of employees when neither expectations or new tactical targets are clear. Many of us are action oriented, and very much want to improve and effect our imprimatur on the organization, but noting this needs to be done typically through others, moderating our pace may be the better part of valor given changes of the group. During this time frame, any changes that are considered can be discussed with the entire group, who may have a different perspective given the new *milieu*. Rather than considering this a threat, it actually is a way to ensure alignment, avoidance of bias, and thoughtful decision-making skills – all keys to good leadership and balance.

A final consideration is that while many of your former peers will be genuinely happy with your new position, others may be less than pleased. They may question your authority, attempt to foment discontent, or be passive aggressive in words or action. As noted earlier, communication after obtaining a firm understanding of the more senior manager expectations is key to strengthen the overall team effort, and identify those who may not be supportive of the needed efforts of the group to fulfill the organizational objectives. By using both group and individual meetings, the technical executive can identify those who are actively contributing to the group effort, and those who are creating dissension and diminishing productivity. It is important, clearly, to identify the latter as soon as possible to deal effectively with such individuals to further investigate their reticence to be part of the team effort, and/or their behavior. Utilizing the strategies noted above for discontented employees can be of significant value, allowing a mutual understanding of whether the direct report can exist in the new structure, or whether another opportunity is more suited to his or her needs.

"My peers say I have made a difference. That means more to me than winning an Oscar".

-Conrad Hall

REFERENCES

Cartwright, T., 2003. Managing Conflict with Peers. Center for Creative Leadership, Greensboro.

Cohen, L., 2012. Murder and Euthanasia Accusations Against Physicians. Mayo Clinic Proceedings 97, 814–816.

Deloitte Consulting LLP with Forbes Insights. Talent Edge 2020: Building the recovery together— What talent expects and how leaders are responding. April 2011.

McKenna, P., Maister, D., 2002. First Among Equals: How to Manage a Group of Professionals. The Free Press, New York.

Steers, R.M., Porter, L.M., 1995. Motivation and Work Behavior. McGraw-Hill, New York.

Relationships: More Than Just Your Specialty

"Because the purpose of business is to create a customer, the business enterprise has two- and only two – basic functions: marketing and innovation. Marketing and innovation produce results; all the rest are costs".

-Peter Drucker

"The most important single ingredient in the formula of success is knowing how to get along with people".

-Theodore Roosevelt

"A year from now you will wish you had started today".

-Karen Lamb

Jeb, the Facilitator Jeb was trained in industrial engineering, and had worked within a manufacturing team improving process flow within the fermentation unit in the firm. He interfaced with a number of groups in the downstream process development group as well as the analytical biochemistry part of the firm, solidifying the working relationships both with individuals and their respective groups to streamline manufacturing output. He had actively expanded his working associations to the downstream processing group, in his effort to move desired efficiencies to the fill and finish part of the organization. Because of his developed network, he began to have further relationships with corporate development that used his expertise as a resource on predicting potential challenges to fulfill orders for the market. Jeb was eventually asked to join the investor relations group, because of his frequent interactions with not only manufacturing and corporate development, but also because he acted as an occasional face to the customer and investment community. Within this role, he was able to work with marketing and sales, product development as well as manufacturing and the corporate group, and continued to expand his network into the complementors of the business, including suppliers, distributors, and investors. He became an internal resource for the firm as manifest by the understanding of both processes and the perspectives of the related external environment. With the transition to a new CEO, Jeb was chosen to head up a new area of the company, corporate strategy, which would be housed within the finance part of the organization. He worked closely with the global head of marketing and sales, as well as the head of research and development to provide a working paradigm to encompass the new CEO's vision for the company. Upon retirement, he had worked in virtually every part of the organization, had relationships throughout the firm, and was known to be able to facilitate teams and processes across diverse functional areas.

COLLABORATION

Jeb was clearly able to work well with his colleagues, and had a clear and fundamental vision initially of how he could impact the organization with his industrial engineering background within manufacturing. A key aspect was his realization that diverse parts of the organization required cooperative efforts, requiring moving into the overlap areas of functional groups. Being able to tie in everything from manufacturing to downstream processing and bioanalytical groups broke down silos and allowed for a potential understanding at the team and group level of more efficient ways to work together. This was translated further as the diversity of interactions widened; Jeb's efforts pushed into involving himself in other areas outside of the classic "science" ones, into more corporate and commercial *milieus*. Collaboration to cooperate, within and outside of the organization, was relevant in improving efficiencies and productivity within the firm, something at which Jeb understood and excelled. Interestingly, Jeb once noted that he never considered himself anything but an engineer, but did note that he liked to be intellectually challenged (challenge career anchor, see Chapter 3), and that the gradual changes from the technical to the corporate provided such an opportunity – "it takes a lot to manage people; you have to think how they feel, you have to think on your feet, and you have to make it work for the company – a lot easier than taking a few months to figure out fermentation conditions". By being able to communicate his ideas, particularly how they would both benefit the various groups he was working with and how they would work within his own group (and management), he was able to identify situations where all could benefit, which was for the best interests of the organization.

Another aspect at which Jeb excelled was his ability to connect with others. He had a sincere interest not only in the functional relationships between the groups within which he was interacting, but also the people in these groups. He took time to understand colleagues both on a personal level as well as a professional one, by noting both personal interests and professional accomplishments, and generated a level of trust by doing so. Although not extroverted, he had the realization that working with others was important to accomplish both his and his teammate's goals, and used one-on-one meetings effectively to create relationships that were very clear at team and group meetings. Indeed, Jeb "exercised" the relationship creating "muscle" in spite of this not being "natural" for him, which then helped strengthen this part of his work persona. As he rose in the organization, he would spend considerable time establishing relationships with his (new) peers, as well as maintaining many of his previous relationships.

LOST IN TRANSLATION

We as technical executives often have to act as translators, not only within our specific areas of the organization, be they engineering, manufacturing, quality, molecular biology, or clinical development, but to others with less or different areas of expertise. The omnipresent challenge is being able to simplify without losing context, and ensuring we are understood (as noted in earlier chapters). The natural tendency that I have seen is to stay within one's own functional area when developing relationships, as communication is easier and there are more common experiences; even in teams, such as product development matrix teams where there is ostensibly more diversity, relationships still are stronger within functional and related areas, often just by association and geographic location of offices. It takes effort and work to ensure that our communications are understood, and that we enhance our working interactions with non-technical personnel. Hence, being busy with our day-to-day responsibilities, often this important role takes on less priority than perhaps it should. However, it has already been mentioned that those projects that have a strong relationship between commercial and technical succeed at a significantly higher rate than those having a suboptimal one; as technical executives, our own emphasis, and the emphasis to make to our groups and teams, is to ensure that we do not fall into the convenience trap of interfacing only with our technical or R&D brethren. While being part of a technical department does indeed facilitate our expertise, and is "inward" facing toward departmental colleagues, our best efforts for the organization are to take the effort to create working relationships outside our functional areas to broaden and share our competencies toward areas of the firm which are more "outward" facing (*e.g.* commercial part of the firm). Similarly, this allows us to learn the perspective of that part of the organization, and facilitates a broader collaborative environment responsive to both internal and external customers. As well, this allows us to communicate better with these colleagues, further facilitating the collaboration.

Indeed, this is often a way that technically trained individuals move from a functional area to a broader, more corporate one; they are relied upon to provide

TABLE 9.1 Translation Principles

Know your audience – avoid patronizing text
Prepare, prepare, prepare – it's hard to simplify, and easy to complicate
Avoid jargon, or if unavoidable, define *a priori*
High level first – fill in details *after* there is assurance of understanding
Ask yourself, would anyone without an engineering/scientific/technical/ manufacturing background understand your presentation? Would a graduate student? Would a college student? (*etc.*)(See line 1.)
Use questions to ascertain understanding, provide more detail, and engender follow up

interpretation between one part of the organization to another in a manner which is neither condescending nor complex. I can recall when called upon from the marketing part of the firm to explain the data and implications of a particular study that had just been completed; my first attempt was done with little preparation, running over from another meeting and utilizing scientific and clinical jargon that left my colleagues confused and very frustrated (see Table 9.1). Having some realization of the error of my ways, I resolved to return to the group the next day, and falling back on my days as an instructor, apologizing profusely about the day before, explained simply the key findings and messages of the data, filling in details when questions were asked, using questions to ensure comprehension, and inviting follow up if subsequent questions arose. This resulted in being requested to present to the business unit head, then the global head of marketing and sales. This helped hone my presentation of the data, and with the questions being asked, made me understand the relative priorities – going from the tactical use in closing sales at the team level, to implications of and fit within a portfolio of assets at the corporate level. Similar to Jeb, this prompted an investigation of challenges in these areas, which led me to work more closely with the commercial part of the organization, and eventually moving over into that part of the firm.

REACHING OUT

Often our ability to initially reach out is as easy as setting up meetings with others in the non-scientific areas of the team or teams we are resident. These are excellent relationships with which to begin because these are typically peer-associated, *viz.* ones which are at the same level within the organization. As such, these will potentially be the individuals with whom one might work for considerable amounts of time – not only on the specific team, but also (and particularly) when moving up in the hierarchy in the firm. These are opportunities to understand better the perspective of different parts of the organization from where we sit, whether that is a different area in research or engineering, product or clinical development, and/ or government or investor relations. Certainly, there are formalized ways in larger organizations that specifically create experiences to be able to practice at skills in different parts of the firm, with the goal of becoming a manager; these can be invaluable for those who definitely have the general manager career anchor. However, establishing relationships at the peer level is a key obligation without such formalized training programs to engender both a more holistic view of the organization within which we dwell, and also to exercise our abilities to learn about the day-to-day activities of other areas which can help to both do our jobs better, and contribute to the organization by having a more pluralistic view of the team. This is especially important in either technological areas or markets that are changing very rapidly and where both monitoring and response may require significant and concerted efforts. Being able to see situations from all different perspectives improves both the ability to make meaningful contributions on the team, as well as decisions affecting not only one's own functional area, but collaterally others as well. Further, this at times may afford not only risk reduction, but changes in outlook from considering something as an uncertainty to a risk (or vice versa; see Chapter 6). Even those who do not aspire toward a management track benefit from expanding both networks and relationships, as diversity on point of view, and the potential of working together on teams in the future, is always a possibility. As technical executives, we need to be aware of this to always provide experiences that might be leveraged for the benefit of the organization both today and tomorrow.

OVERLAPPING INTERESTS

As noted, a key aspect of creating relationships is to better understand the views of others within the organization who may have different perspectives (and cultures); moreover, they may also while speaking the same language mean something very different (*e.g.* having "confidence" in information means something quite different when said by staff from engineering compared with investor relations). By interacting, one can become accustomed to these subtleties to the benefit of the team and/or group, and thus the organization.

In addition to garnering an understanding of other parts of the firm, one can begin to find overlapping interests between different groups. Interestingly, this is a particular strength of the technical manager/executive, since the analytical mindset often found in these areas of the firm can be quite valuable when directed toward such an activity – as noted in Chapter 1, "connecting the dots" vis-à-vis technology and innovation is a key responsibility of technical executives. Applying this to diverse groups inside and outside of R&D is a key skill in order to both create positive working relationships as well as discover value creating opportunities within the organization. Teams routinely meet in order to monitor and report progress, create strategies, and construct tactics of their respective projects; this microcosm of the company is an effective way to identify overlapping interests at the project level, which is a useful paradigm more broadly within the organization. We as technical and scientific executives can utilize this despite not being on teams to lead both our groups as well as interface with others, whether this is formalized in corporate task forces, *ad hoc* committees, or staff meetings with our superiors, as well as more informal settings, when working with peers outside our immediate functional areas. Taking advantage of an analytical mindset to identify common interests can pay significant dividends for the organization.

Moreover, and importantly, proactively looking for overlapping interests is relevant when dealing with potential conflict between groups, identifying early areas of potential tension, or facilitating solutions if in the midst thereof. It has been shown in a variety of different studies (see References) that one of the first aspects to evaluate in any conflict situation is the interests of the parties involved, including common or shared interests (which *a priori* may not be apparent) and ones that differ. This begins a process of considerations of the priorities of such interests, from ones that are minor to the "third rail" issues. In fact, this particular area is one having considerable importance to any new technical executive, *viz.* negotiation. While perhaps not readily apparent to the casual observer, particularly with in R&D, this is a key skill to either obtain or enhance as one moves from being an individual performer in the lab to working actively with others in the organization. Indeed, almost all of our interactions can be considered negotiations of one form or another, whether advocating for resources or presenting at the board level; we are advocating a particular point of view in order to communicate, inform, and/or convince others of our perspective. Training in negotiation is invaluable, as it not only emphasizes utilizing our skills in identifying overlaps, but also forces us to prepare for interactions with others, attempting to understand the stakeholders in any decision/interaction/issue, potential walk-away points, best alternatives, understanding objectives, having legitimate facts to support our perspectives (and predicting those from other perspectives), based on a relationship and communication between those involved. While not all of these interactions are "negotiations" in the classic sense or in context of conflict, they can be informed by thinking about the situation in a way that searches for solutions *via* interests and outcomes, which may be stepwise in format.

I can recall when I served on a commercialization task force, leading a subgroup that involved interfacing with the R&D group at the company. These particular groups had never before had any level of corporate or commercial reachback into their respective areas; they had been considered "too early" in the development value chain to have any requirement for commercial interest. Moreover, both group heads were clearly unaccustomed to having commercial groups interface with their groups. My initial meetings with them were quite tense, and it took some time for each to open up and allow me to investigate their respective interests; it required establishing a relationship of trust (facilitated by being a former R&D leader), and communicating in a way that avoided business jargon but introduced concepts in a way that afforded them respect to their accomplishments and intelligence without being patronizing. What I discovered was that, clearly, given the lack of attention that had been paid to this part of the organization within commercialization, there was a perceived threat that marketing would be "telling us what to do", rather than being connected in a way that provided an overall sense of direction to the firm. Articulating the interests of the organization's commercial and corporate group, and finding the commonalities *first* before introducing changes, provided a huge opportunity to create value. In fact, the paradigm of providing general targets for R&D (*e.g.* therapeutic areas), while allowing complete freedom and flexibility to achieve such, combined with the commercial group understanding that knowledge generation (*e.g.* innovation) is implicitly different conceptually, with different timelines – especially early in the process, diminished any perceived threat to the research groups. By using a negotiation approach with the R&D groups,

---

At the Speed of Sound: Predicting Outcomes from Conversational Dynamics Within the First 5 Minutes

First impressions have been shown in a variety of different studies to have a large impact on overall short- and long-term judgments – indeed, from evaluation of professors and teachers to job interviews and outcome of court cases, "thin slices" of time (initially reported at 30 seconds and subsequently found as short as 6 seconds) have been found to be predictive in future evaluations of instructors. These microcosms of time have been shown to be predictive in situations of marital research, where observation of the first 3 minutes of a conflict can predict future outcome of divorce; 5 minutes of observation has been used to predict outcomes such as criminal conviction and professional competency as well – despite outcomes being some time in the future. Curnhan and Pentland showed that conversational dynamics play a large role in these outcomes, using a simulated negotiation between a VP and middle manager on a compensation package, analyzed by computer algorithms evaluating *engagement* (turn taking in speaking), *proportion of time speaking, mirroring* (repeating or acknowledging the other speaker), and *prosodic emphasis* (*i.e.* emotional speech). Findings differed depending on the status within an organization: increases in success in negotiation with increased proportion of speaking time were found for VP level managers, but not middle managers. Vocal mirroring was positively associated with economic success by middle managers but not VPs; prosodic emphasis in general was associated with poorer outcomes for both groups. Interestingly, there was no difference on engagement between VP and middle manager level individuals, and there were no differences ascribed to gender of either VP or middle managers on the results. These data suggest that there are specific conversational dynamics to be considered that may predict relative outcomes in negotiation or negotiation-type situations.

Curhan JR, Pentland A. Thin Slices of Negotiation: Predicting Outcomes from Conversational Dynamics Within the First 5 Minutes. Journal of Applied Psychology 92:802-811, 2007.

the commercialization initiative was able to improve the overall organizational productivity and portfolio management process, where these groups became integrated and actively participated within value chain initiatives.

DEALING WITH DISTANCE

Our organizations, no matter how small or diverse, are part of a global economy and system transcending geographies or time zones and require both an understanding of culture and (to a certain extent) language to collaborate effectively. We as technical executives and managers often can communicate with our colleagues in the language of our respective sciences, providing a modicum of fundamental understanding. As we move toward more general responsibilities we need to ensure that we have a breadth of experience to ensure that not only is information transferred, but also true communication and relationships are established. "Distance", a shorthand for cultural, time, and language differences, has become a reality for both junior and senior members of the team and organization, requiring even more effort to ensure our relationships are established and nurtured.

Today, we have a myriad of mechanisms to attempt to stay connected to our colleagues and collaborators – email, social media, video conferences, Skype, telecons, webex *etc.* all allow a level of communication unprecedented from the days of connecting by a daisy-chain phone conference. However, it is very clear that even within this context, the geographic distances as noted earlier of only 50 meters diminish significantly the interaction of one team member to another, and a difference of a floor essentially removes all interaction with the exception of group/team meetings (see Allen and Henn, References). Interestingly, even with the myriad of communication devices noted, the data show that *any* use of communication diminishes based on distance, and that the general pattern of communication is always the same – it is not differentiated by opportunity, but by distance; the closer we are to someone (again, noting the 50 meters) the better chance we will interact with them *via* multiple modes of communication. It is thus vitally important that we take the initiative to design our interactions proactively, in order to establish the relationships needed to be productive at the team and group level. To a certain extent, this makes individuals from multinational companies "telecommuters", as we may not see the contributors to the team efforts on a daily or frequent basis, due to the dispersed nature of the team (*e.g.* project management in La Jolla, information technology support in Hyderabad, engineering in Rome, program executive in Manchester, and manufacturing in Shenyang). Recent data from telecommuters should thus be valuable for our new teams (Elsbach et al., References) – early establishment of team relationships at the beginning of the project/program, with at least one set of individuals who know each other, and periodic in-person meetings to strengthen the relationships between team members. Moreover, a particularly relevant aspect is the need for all and particularly the team leadership (and technical executive) to constantly probe and anticipate potential issues or conflicts early and often to avoid the snowball effect of misunderstanding that can occur in these distance relationships. This will also ensure that at least a minimum understanding of true cultural differences – not necessarily stereotypes, but overall differences in working relationships, such as those profiled between engineers in Germany and France (as in Airbus; see References) – that can affect the way the team works. Paying attention to the details such as which group needs to stay late or start early in the morning, and making sure that these are equitable, often creates a working *milieu* much appreciated by the team members across the globe. Indeed, as a junior, newly appointed team leader with participants around the globe, a team member approached me on the first day of my tenure complaining of the early AM meetings needed to be performed due to the time zone differences between the U.S. and the UK; the previous team leader was from Germany, and despite being in the U.S. always defaulted to very early morning hours for team meetings to accommodate European colleagues. When this issue was broached with the UK team members, issues around traffic, daylight, and inconvenience for the occasional need to bring in *ad hoc* members from the Netherlands were brought up. While the initial approach was to gather information, gradually most (but not all) team members from all sides, just by bringing up the issue with a change in team leadership, began to understand that to be fair, we needed to rotate the times to show a modicum of respect for all team members. While there were still some complaints, overall the vast majority of the team adapted well to rotating schedules, and my travelling to various geographies to lead the meetings from the most inconvenienced part of the team was also helpful. While this may not be possible for all situations, showing a level of concern for all team members did provide better team dynamics with fairly little otherwise overt intervention.

"Anticipate the difficult by managing the easy".

-Lao Tzu

REFERENCES

Allen, T., Henn, G., 2006. The Organization and Architecture of Innovation: Managing the Flow of Technology. Butterworth, New York.

Elsbach, K.D., Cable, D.M., Sherman, J.W., 2010. How Passive 'Face Time' Affects Perceptions of Employees: Evidence of Spontaneous Trait Inference. Human Relations 63, 735–760.

Fisher, R., Ury, W.L., Patton, B., 2011. Getting to Yes: Negotiating without Giving In. Penguin, New York.

Liang, B., 2013. Sidebar: Talking Different Languages: Strategic Issues and the Airbus A380. Chapter 5: Portfolio Management, The Pragmatic MBA for Scientific and Technical Executives. Academic Press, New York.

Tactics: the 4 Ps, and Walk Arounds

"Negative feedback is better than none. I would rather have a man hate me than overlook me. As long as he hates me I make a difference".

-Hugh Prather

"I think it's very important to have a feedback loop, where you're constantly thinking about what you've done and how you could be doing it better".

-Elon Musk

"The most effective way to do it, is to do it".

-Amelia Earhart

Second Chances Ryan was ready to leave the company when his new supervisor was hired; he had been an excellent engineer when he had started with the firm, and had stellar credentials; in his previous job he not only had designed the project management tool that pulled together diverse groups within the organization to a common platform, he had acted as the group leader to effect its initial implementation. Looking to diversify his experiences, he had joined the firm in a junior leadership position, heading a small group, where he was to implement a larger form of the tool he had developed. His first supervisor was a legacy from another smaller company acquired recently (and not his hiring manager), with only a minimum of experience in managing others. When hired, Ryan expected to be able to implement his system as he had previously, but found that his supervisor had much different ideas; she felt it necessary to

Managing and Leading for Science Professionals. http://dx.doi.org/10.1016/B978-0-12-416686-8.00010-4

question each action and plan that Ryan had put together, despite articulating his previous experiences elsewhere. By report, their one-on-one meetings began with notations of what had not been done since the last meeting, and notations of what needed to be performed, which were documented responsibilities of his supervisor, and did not involve either implementation of the project management system or the other projects in his job description. When he complained to the human resources representative of the department, he was told that upon inquiry his supervisor was delegating to him, and that he should be pleased that he had been trusted with responsibility. When Ryan noted that when he finished these tasks his supervisor not only took credit for these but also embellished any actions or results, Ryan was asked to address this directly with his supervisor. With this, Ryan confided in his colleagues that he intended to leave. However, with the hiring of a new Senior Vice President of Product Engineering, Ryan was moved to a new section on Program Management, with a new supervisor just hired from the largest company in the industry. This new supervisor (a Vice President) was also putting together systems in order to create an infrastructure allowing better communication and oversight; he asked Ryan to work with him to integrate their systems in order to maximize the benefits and avoid conflicts of these systems. Ryan and his supervisor worked collaboratively and modernized the department and the working project management systems over the next year, creating an efficient system allowing for senior management communication as well as program management across departments. When the program was implemented, Ryan's supervisor asked him to present this to the entire management team. As a result, in distinction to leaving the company, Ryan became the Vice President of Program Management when his supervisor was appointed to a corporate position.

BEING SENSITIVE TO THE INDIVIDUAL WITHIN A BROAD FOCUS

As managers of technology, scientific and technologic executives have a daunting task: we must be able to recognize progress as well as potential disrupters, and develop projects that meet the needs of a constantly evolving marketplace. The requisite skills necessary for this revolve around at least a modicum of scientific sophistication in order to at least converse at a level that provides not only the ability to ask appropriate questions, but to guide on the basis of corporate needs. This engenders a large amount of responsibility to tie together knowledge generation, response to commercial needs, and meeting of corporate objectives.

Within this as has been much discussed is the need to work with others to accomplish these goals. One of the most challenging components is the manner by which we think not only about our broad mandate, but also on how we might operationalize these tasks, particularly in our interactions with our teams, groups, or departments, as appropriate. Indeed, it could be argued that this is

one of the most relevant components of our jobs, as it is the day-to-day manifestation of our thought processes derived from direction we ourselves receive;
it is *our* execution to create value for the organization.

Hence, our one-on-one meetings with reports are particularly important in
this regard. While task orientation and delegation is of high importance, we
need to ensure there is a balanced approach that includes not only the data but
the "soft stuff" as well – an understanding of the concept that our actions need
to be manifest by others, and that we should clearly pay attention to the needs
of the members of our groups. While not in exclusion to the activities ensuring
that our groups remain productive, a tantamount effort should be considered for
ensuring the individual team members are being "fed and watered", with the
latter oftentimes creating the *milieu* for the former.

Ryan's interaction with his first manager was at best problematic for a
variety of different reasons, but at least some issues were based on a lack
of a balanced approach by his supervisor. While the supervisor seemed to
understand the technology that Ryan had developed, asking presumably pertinent questions during their meetings, and was delegating responsibility to
him, it was not perceived by Ryan as being either helpful or useful. In fact,
his complaints to the HR department suggested that he was not seeing this as
a development opportunity being provided. Instead, Ryan was considering
leaving because he felt his efforts were being credited to others, and that the
responsibilities for which he believed he was hired were being both questioned and to a certain extent, being ignored. So while his supervisor was
directing him toward certain tasks, and was delegating to him towards higher
level responsibilities (*e.g.* those which were within her area), it was not perceived to be for the good of the entire organization, but rather centralized
around the supervisor. Whether these perceptions were true or not may have
reflected Ryan's own bias, but clearly this was interfering with his adding
value to the organization.

"Be nice to people on your way up because you'll meet them on your way down".

-Wilson Mizner

TACTICAL POINTS: INDIVIDUAL MEETINGS

While the style and situations of meetings with the individuals that one is managing cannot and should not be scripted, clearly there are areas that should be
at least covered based on responsibilities of the group. Ryan's supervisor was
focused on tasks that had/had not been performed, which can be an important
component within any one-on-one meeting. Further, there was an apparent
delegation of responsibility as well during these meetings, which can be quite
appropriate if there is clear articulation of the goals of the responsibility and
authority provided. However, there is value in encompassing more areas than
just ones manifesting programs or projects. Indeed, my experience has been that

TABLE 10.1 The Four Ps for Individual Meetings

Projects/Programs	Progress on areas of responsibility
Personnel	Status of direct reports; satisfaction, issues or concerns
Personal	Status of individual report; satisfaction; issues or concerns; progress toward personal goals
Personal II	Feedback to supervisor; "What could I be doing better? What are you afraid I might do?"

bringing in a more structured involvement and perspective of other areas does materially affect both the relationship between the manager and team member, with, paradoxically, also a level of flexibility at the same time that can be adapted to different situations. Ryan obviously did not respond well to the initial expectations and style of his first manager, but was able to flourish under his subsequent one, underlining that the ability to understand needs of team members by managers can have powerful influences on motivation and performance. It is finding what those needs are that can be largely valuable to the relationship, productivity, and the organization at large.

Hence, when having individual meetings with team members and/or direct reports, as a rule I have found that covering minimally the "four Ps" has helped at least ensure that I understand both technical progress as well as personal concerns. While this by no means is necessarily all encompassing, it does provide a modicum of understanding that at least, when used consistently, allows both a high-level conceptual checklist for the programs and projects, and the team member as an individual. Such an approach has helped me not ignore, upon my haste to achieve certain tasks, the person in front of me and his or her needs. For me, the four Ps encompass program/projects; personnel; personal; and personal II. These will be further elaborated on below, and are summarized in Table 10.1.

PROJECTS/PROGRAMS

In this category, the specific progress of the projects and programs that are the responsibility of the direct report are discussed. This is in particular of importance for not only the identification of milestones of the specific projects, but also provides an opportunity for an understanding of the resource needs of the individual to facilitate progress of his or her particular programs of responsibility. Indeed, it is often helpful to structure information exchange on the basis of several questions, initially around what is the objective, whether it is a target, an action, or an outcome; in this way, there is agreement on the subject matter at hand and clear understanding by both parties of that which is being discussed. Next, specific articulation on whether the program is ahead, behind, or on schedule (and the inherent reasons as such) fundamentally identifies a level of urgency or concern that is attached to the progress of the program. Next, the ensuing discussion would revolve around the actions taken, and importantly, the outcome and any lessons learned from the activities that not only apply to the project, but that might be applicable more broadly. Finally, these progress reports on the projects and programs should identify the next stage of action, and whether any additional resources are required for accomplishment, as well as any modifications of the timelines potentially being required. An important component of this part of the one-on-one is the ability to ensure frank and clear communication between supervisor and employee in the update, in order both to understand accomplishments but also potential resources that will be required for the program. As a key responsibility of the supervisor, the provision of resources should be offered *de rigeur* as team members may be reticent to ask due to perceptions of failure or other fears that might reflect on assessments of competence. Nonetheless, for both the development of the programs as well as the employees, we as technical executives must be cognizant of such needs in order to maximize the potential of both.

"But innovation comes from people meeting up in the hallways or calling each other at 10:30 at night with a new idea, or because they realized something that shoots holes in how we've been thinking about a problem".

-Steve Jobs

PERSONNEL

As has been noted in earlier chapters, a key responsibility of technical executives is to ensure that we have empowered our teams and reports, in order to be certain that they continue to feel motivated and appreciated for their efforts, as well as for development of their skills both technically as well as managerially. In turn, we need to ensure that these efforts translate further down the line toward the efforts our individual reports effect for their respective teams – it is the appropriate extension of our mentorship to the mentorship of others, and is a key responsibility for us as managers to further management skills in our groups. Ryan's initial supervisor seemed to be trying at least by report to create a set of managerial expectations by delegation, although her efforts seemed to not extend to any team members reporting to Ryan, and were focused more on delegation of tasks (as opposed to responsibilities and authority) to him. Ryan did not respond well to these efforts, and there did not seem to be the requisite understanding of importance of this area by either the supervisor or Ryan himself. Making sure that we pay attention not only to our individual reports but also one layer (or more!) further into the organization emphasizes the importance we as technical executives place on this area, sending a clear message of what is expected for those in our respective groups, and thus creating a transparent and open organization. I have often found that direct questioning around the motivational mood of the group is a way to evaluate how the team below the direct report is being perceived, and further, asking why the tone is good, bad, or indifferent can provide an open-ended way to determine the efforts of the individual on fostering motivation, or at least taking the time to understand what the group tenor may be. Particularly for new technical reports, anecdote has been that this needs to be introduced in a non-threatening but constant manner – often these are questions that have not been posed to technical personnel in the past, which in contrast has typically focused on project updates alone. Nonetheless, a consistent pattern of addressing our "report's reports" demonstrates both interest and clear importance that provides a clear expectation to be able to comment both how and why there is a specific perception. Moreover, it can provide important information to both managers on the current mood of the department/division, potentially identifying areas that need to be addressed by either/both.

An important aspect of this area is to avoid both the perception and the reality of micromanagement. As noted, this revolves around treating others as merely an arm of the supervisor, rather than allowing reports and team members to come up with their own solutions to challenges encountered or delegated to them. This is a fine line needing to be fully considered by the technical executive in order to avoid creating demotivation while trying to be motivating at the same time! Feedback will be important to understand whether this is the case (see below); however, one should be very cognizant of this as a possibility. Indeed, I can recall one case where as a technical manager I was perceived as "meddling"; the situation was one where I asked about a specific individual who reported to one of my directors; he was nondescript about the individual, and when further questioned asked me directly whether she had come to me to discuss him. When I noted that she had not, he told me that he would prefer me "not to meddle in the situation", an obvious red flag for further discussion. Upon further probing, there had been apparent friction between the two, and my director was doing the best he could to manage the situation, although not to the point of either bringing me or the HR department into the situation. Once I clarified my role as supportive and non-adversarial, but rather looking out for the best interests of the department, he felt more comfortable, and indeed, ended up managing the situation quite well, although needing to have HR involved in the end. It is thus important to both be supportive in situations where managerial skills are being exercised and developed, although ensuring that the overall organization is supported as well.

"When I finally got a management position, I found out how hard it is to lead and manage people".

-Guy Kawasaki

PERSONAL

Taking interest in direct reports has been covered throughout many of the chapters herein, but some points should be emphasized. On an annual basis reviewing goals for the coming year should be *de rigueur* and familiar to most executives; however, in addition, asking the question of where the individual would like to be at a time further in the future – 3, 5, and/or 10 years – should also be discussed, and the perceived experiences that would be necessary to achieve these long-term goals. At each one-on-one meeting, reviewing progress towards those goals for the year, and those goals further into the future, should be discussed, and whether experiences to date and expected would be relevant to the longer term goals. These discussions are important because it allows active participation in career development of the individual, provides the supervisor with an understanding of the interests of the report, and allows both to create a plan to address both the needs of the individual and how these can fit into the organizational needs (or not, as the case may be). It also helps both the supervisor and the team member become aware of their specific career anchors (see Chapter 3). Having employees understand they are moving toward their agreed upon goals is indeed motivational, and tends towards creating dedicated team members who become passionate in what they do. When current opportunities do not necessarily allow for all of the needed experiences for individual employees, we can still either find outside opportunities, substitute opportunities, or redirect toward other areas that might also be in the interests of the individual. The same goes for those reports who have a desire to achieve a certain position or set of responsibilities, but which may not exist in the firm; both providing guidance to such an employee of the limited experiences that could allow for achievement of at least part of his or her goals is important, as well as opportunities that could act as surrogates is also an important part of helping plan our reports' career development, to the extent by which resources are available. Such attention to these areas should be integrated if possible into the other areas of delegation, motivation, and direction as part of the personal aspects addressed in regular meetings.

"The secret to winning is constant, consistent management".

-Tom Landry

PERSONAL II

I have always found, ironically, that in my one-on-one sessions, the person who benefits most is me. I do not believe this is because I have not been sensitive to the needs or resource requirements of my direct reports, or been dominant about the interaction reflecting my requirements as opposed to those of the direct report. In fact, usually a relatively small amount of time is dedicated to this component, but one I always address, *viz.* feedback. Oftentimes, particularly as one rises through an organization or in title, the level of feedback decreases due to lack of opportunity, a limited number of interactions with other managers, or frank time constraints limiting discussion as such (nonetheless, see Chapter 11, Leading and Mentoring Yourself). Hence, obtaining feedback on one's performance can often be difficult, particularly within the areas where one has direct responsibility. As a result, being able to ask one's direct reports is an important manifestation of leadership, and as well, motivating for team members. Just as delegation encompasses trust between the supervisor and employee, being able to give feedback from the position of the employee to the supervisor takes a great deal of trust, in that frank commentary will not be taken either as an attack or as fodder for the supervisor against the employee. It does certainly take time to create a level of trust that will best make asking for feedback a valuable discourse within a one-on-one meeting, but is well worth the effort to fundamentally understand from rank and file the perception of us as technical executives, how we are doing and where we might need to improve. As well, it undoubtedly can be used as we have our own meetings with our supervisors, providing both data and evidence of our willingness to seek commentary about our own performance. Addressing what we might do better can shed light on our blind spots to either improve or seek assistance if needed, and understand at least a perspective about performance within our part of the organization. This also makes providing feedback to a supervisor less threatening when addressed in this way.

In addition, understanding potential fears from the group or members thereof is an important aspect of feedback. Asking directly if there is anything that is either thought to be problematic or which the team feels is ill-advised can provide a significant amount of information about perceptions of not only the supervisor but the management team of which he or she is a member. Again, in the context of asking about how one could do better, this question and approach can be non-threatening to one's direct reports, particularly as trust strengthens between the supervisor and employee. These questions often can give surprising replies as well. I have heard statements of, "I want your job" on what a director wants to do in five years, to "Everyone is scared you're going to take away the [individual serving] coffee maker – that would be a real demotivator and might cause a revolt". Notwithstanding these frank and honest comments, excellent feedback has been given around what to maintain in the portfolio, challenges seen on the horizon, opportunities in other parts of the organization as well as managing growth. Having these questions really does allow an open-ended and broad conversation that can be very revealing around what is important to both the individual employee as well as the perceptions of the team of the supervisor. Of note is that oftentimes these types of questions do not go over well in a more public forum; feedback can be very limited in a situation when one's peers (or other supervisors) are gathered in one room/meeting; it can be quite threatening, and just the lack of certainty on what is the most appropriate action due to presumed unspoken norms can cause paralysis of action while looking to others for cues ("pluralistic ignorance"). Hence, while these approaches can work quite well in a one-on-one situation, they may work less well in a more open forum, particularly with those who might be more introverted in nature.

"Everybody needs feedback, and it's a heck of a lot cheaper than paying a trainer".

-Doug Lowenstein

BEING VISIBLE

It is no exaggeration to note that while science is universal, technology development is local, and requires a fundamental understanding of the cultural, political, corporate, and other pressures and interactions that occur within any organization, in addition to expertise in science and engineering. Hence, this represents a challenge for any set of technical executives, as directing R&D (as well as other areas) from remote locations with limited interaction can be compared to the allegorical Platonic cave – what we think or what we hear may merely be shadows and not be reality or what was intended by either the supervisor or the team members. All need to understand that the *milieu* within which we work has distinct qualities, requiring us to ensure what we believe to be a current situation is reality and not just those shadows on the wall. For technical executives, this engenders being visible within the group and team, *viz.* not only being seen and present, but also being available, approachable, and willing to garner information and feedback in both formal and especially informal settings. In the past, this has been noted as "management by walking around" or other similar monikers; while more recently maligned because of the practice of staged "scheduled random" interactions, in fact when performed in a way that team members do not believe to be rote, can have exceptional benefits. This provides the rank and file as well as the manager excellent feedback, especially if done in a way that is fact finding (not attempting to criticize), informal, and provides a level of recognition for those who engage and provide input into the day-to-day as well as higher level aspects of the organization. Further, particularly in the cases where there are unanswered questions or issues, being able to provide feedback and follow up as a supervisor strengthens the relationship with team members, and enhances credibility within the division and the management team. In this way, not only does the supervisor build rapport with the team, but also to a certain extent garners information with less filtering, particularly important when at very high levels in the organization. While any filtering cannot be entirely avoided due to issues of position, it can at least provide a level of feedback particularly when trust has been established. Indeed, I have seen the CEO of a large multi-national firm fire a senior vice president whose direct supervisor did not take action, despite a myriad of complaints from several team leaders of capricious behavior and favoritism, based on interaction with several team leaders during an informal contact. While often we as managers are so busy that we are "chained to the desk", to avoid any perception of the office tower, it is the obligation of technical executives to minimize the "boundary impedance" of having an open door policy and expect our teams to come to us; we need to be proactive in interaction to ensure that we understand the *milieu*, and that direction is clear and communication is facilitated.

"The biggest cowards are managers who don't let people know where they stand".

-Jack Welch

REFERENCES

Drucker, P.F., 1993. Managing in Turbulent Times. HarperBusiness, New York.

Drucker, P.F., 2006. The Effective Executive: The Definitive Guide to Getting the Right Things Done (Revised). HarperCollins, New York.

Peters, T.J., Waterman, R.H., 2004. In Search of Excellence: Lessons from America's Best-Run Companies. HarperCollings, New York.

Pulakos, E.D., 2009. Performance Management: A New Approach for Driving Business Results. John Wiley & Sons, New York.

Leading and Managing Yourself: Mentors

"Mentor: Someone whose hindsight can become your foresight".

-Unknown

"The time to repair the roof is when the sun is shining".

-John F. Kennedy

"Instead of waiting for someone to take you under his wing, go out and find a wing to climb under".

-Dave Thomas

Docendo Discimus (Learn by Teaching) Dave's experiences were from some of the largest companies in the industry, where he had moved up in the ranks because of his technical knowledge and ability to translate information gleaned from the literature into his everyday responsibilities within operations. His perspective was unique, in that he not only was thoughtful about the scientific aspects of his job, but took every opportunity to determine the relative benefits from a cost perspective in all his suggested actions or initiatives, perhaps due to his double major in college in both biology and economics. In addition, he had a natural propensity for assisting others, having played basketball at a varsity level as a guard in his Division III school, and in high school before that. After being promoted to a senior manager, he actively sought out what he called "coaching" from others outside his department, in order to further improve upon his performance. Dave began regularly meeting with two other more experienced managers, who provided feedback and guidance to questions and articulated thoughts around operations, management, and career progression, both prompted by Dave as well as his mentors. After about a year of such meetings, Dave (with the wholehearted support of his coaches) asked his supervisor that he be considered for the company sponsored MBA program at the local university; he outlined not only his background, but his overall career aims and his discussions with his mentors. He provided a rationale for both continuing to work at the organization during this time, his planned contributions, and how this would assist in achieving his career goals. His supervisor was impressed with the thoroughness of his presentation as well as determination of the needs specific for his career goals, and supported Dave as he applied, was accepted, and completed the program. As promised, Dave continued to work within the department, and helped create a simple monitoring tool for the department allowing for all team members to understand where their projects were at any given timeframe, linked to the target product profile. Dave continued meeting with his mentors, and added another within corporate development; he began shifting his emphasis towards the more commercial aspects of the organization. When offered an opportunity to lead a new spin-out venture, he accepted the position, as he had discussed this with his mentors as a natural area of career progression for him. Dave continued within this position, growing the business toward profitability, and continued his interactions with his mentors, adding several more as he moved through different challenges of the new business. He once wrote to one of his mentors, "Thank you so much for the advice and conversations. You've shaped my experience in ways I never would have imagined having on my own". Dave noted that he himself had actively begun mentoring others, even as his new spin-out was starting, to "give back and learn".

Mentor, from the Greek character from *The Odyssey*, can be defined in a variety of ways, but fundamentally reflects a typically more experienced individual who can use both your and their experiences to help you move forward both professionally and socially. Good mentors are willing to take the time to share their knowledge and experience in such a way that as mentees, we gain from these lessons without potentially suffering the consequences ourselves, or we learn additional insights from those we do suffer firsthand. While almost axiomatic that good mentors are busy people, with their own set of responsibilities, commitments, and activities, somehow they always make time for developing others; indeed, they recognize the importance of both the next generation moving up the ranks as well as the previous generation of those who helped them succeed. Indeed, good mentors often convey the attitude that they themselves recall when they were in the mentee's place, both literally and figuratively, and are empathetic to these situations. Combined with feedback from both supervisors and reports/team members, mentorship provides an excellent opportunity for personal and professional development.

TRAITS OF GOOD MENTORS

Worthwhile mentors do not believe mentorship an inconvenience, but rather have genuine concern and desire to improve others. Broadly, people who mentor not only readily share their own lessons learned from their experiences, they are enthusiastic in providing support during situations and difficulties their mentees may be experiencing, and as noted, take time out of their own busy schedules to do so. Mentors have the requisite skills and experiences that allow them to provide advice credibly, and use this to aid their mentees, with genuine desire to help them succeed without any personal gain. They are able to acknowledge and celebrate successes of those with whom they have a relationship, and able to provide honest feedback when perhaps actions were suboptimal. Moreover, such feedback is never derogatory, but constructive. Finally, good mentors allow for active exchange of opinions and data, with the ability to provide thoughtful responses when situations change or new facts come into the picture; they are not relegated to dogma, but challenge both their mentees and themselves to provide opportunities for learning.

More specifically, mentors care about the mentee and his or her success, and act accordingly; this includes providing honest feedback in a way that sometimes is brutal, but at the same time with a manner that is meant to be constructive and helpful rather than punitive. This is particularly important as a teaching and management lesson, as while the latter *may* work – in the Pavlovian sense, when immediate and severe – it results in risk aversion, poor morale, and demotivation. Often, when this type of situation occurs, it is due to the mentor having less interest in the relationship – it may have been forced upon him or her, because of the experiences they may have had in the past, and/or the position held in the organization. However, it is clear that these traits alone are often not sufficient to create a mentorship relationship, and only frank interaction can determine whether such rapport can exist (see below, *Finding a Mentor*).

It is self-evident, then, that good mentors are motivating, not only in support of any efforts being made personally or professionally, but within the context of expansiveness; a good mentor sees and communicates potential that mentees have not seen or even imagined. As Dave noted in his communication to one of his mentors, he was shaped by experiences that he "never would have imagined having on [his] own". Mentors believe in their mentees, often more than the mentees believe in themselves, and find ways to bring out the traits and qualities that help in the development process of the individual. Dave was on point when he called these people his "coaches"; for those who have been involved in activities that have used coaches (*e.g.* athletics), one sees the same type of relationship – helping develop the mindset and skills to perform at the highest level.

The Underdog: John Irving

John Irving is the author of 18 books, numerous short stories, and has had a number of his works made into movies. It would not be unexpected to assume that he was a gifted writer and reader of literature, particularly given the depth of his prose and the volumes of works. However, in fact, he was a poor student, barely passing English, flunking Latin, and requiring significant effort to pass Spanish due

Continued

The Underdog: John Irving—cont'd

to his dyslexia. Irving was also a wrestler, and to his own admission, had "limitations as an athlete". It was his coach, Ted Seabrooke, who taught him lessons on the mat that he subsequently translated to the rest of his schoolwork and his life. Coach Seabrooke noted that Irving would never be better than "halfway decent", but by compensating for his shortcomings, he could still be competitive. In this vein, Irving wrote that he learned how to be especially dedicated, and study not only the physical skills of the sport, but be a true student of the sport as well. He conceptually labeled himself the "underdog", and utilized that moniker in everything he did. While he studied the different positions and approaches of wrestling, he also attempted to take control of matches and put himself in a position not to lose. In his schoolwork, he put in the same preparation: "If my classmates could read our history assignment in an hour, I allowed myself two or three. If I couldn't learn to spell, I would keep a list of my most frequently misspelled words – and I kept the list with me...[I] needed to drill it, over and over again...I began to take my lack of talent seriously". By this approach, he finished his high school career at Phillips Exeter in five years, and completed his first novel at the age of 26, being elected into the American Academy of Arts and Letters in 2001. He was inducted into the National Wrestling Hall of Fame in Stillwater, Oklahoma, in 1992.

Irving J. Underdog. In: Coach: 25 Writers Reflect on People Who Made a Difference. (Blauner A, ed.) Boston, Warner Books, 2005.

As extension, mentors will do their best to prevent their respective mentees from giving up, whether on a project, program, challenge, and especially on themselves. They can bring in their own experiences, and often those of other anonymous mentees or direct reports, with similar situations and circumstances, and the approaches taken, noting those that were successful and those that were not. It is at these challenging times where the mentorship relationship can take considerable time, particularly given the need for feedback and responses. Nonetheless, this points to a key aspect of the mentor–mentee relationship: regular access. By providing set aside time, the mentor shows his or her willingness to provide the needed support and guidance, whether during a key challenge, or as an ongoing developmental relationship. I have seen some would-be excellent mentors with the best of intentions fail on this particular point, to the detriment of the mentee and the relationship; while the advice provided during the time of interaction is sage, the lack of forethought with regards to planning interactions on both parties resulted in a relationship that provided only minimal support, to the point of falling away after a short period of time. While there are different considerations on the mentor–mentee relationship, the most optimal is when the mentee reaches out, and both support the relationship actively. As is often the case, the mentor has more experience in these relationships, and needs to inculcate the mentee with appropriate behaviors to maintain the support. Nonetheless, mentees with more knowledge and experience should be active in ensuring regular interactions take place; more experienced mentors should attempt to facilitate the relationship if they perceive their mentees to require some level of initial support.

The Mentorship Programme: Indian Institute of Technology

The Indian Institute of Technology (IIT) is one of the most prestigious sets of universities in the world. These public engineering schools have very low acceptance rates, being reported to be less than one for every fifty applicants. As part of the ongoing training of students who are accepted into the IIT system, each student is assigned a mentor within the Mentorship Programme sponsored by the Alumni Association. These programs are meant to provide fledgling students with the opportunity of support and guidance by graduates of the schools, based on common goals and career interests. Each student is matched with an appropriate mentor, who volunteers to the program. Because of the relative inexperience of most students with such a process – which is in addition to the standard academic advising for all students – there are guidelines put in place to assist and structure the student "protégé" interaction with the alumni mentor, including registration for the program, instructions around meeting mentors (including interactions for those whose mentors are outside the immediate area of the school), duration, and focus. There is active feedback encouraged from both students and mentors, with mentors being expected to be available, enthusiastic, and supportive of the students, and the students communicating honestly and frankly about the skills, knowledge and goals of interest. Literally thousands of students have participated in this program from different campuses within India, which has not only strengthened the preparation of students for the professional world, but enhanced the relationship of the alumni with their respective schools.

The Mentorship Program, Indian Institute of Technology Kharagpur.
Mentorship.iitkgp.ernet.in

Mentorship also involves continuing the growth and development of the *mentor* as well as the mentee. This is part and parcel of the willingness to seek out and learn and/or garner other education, whether this is from new experiences, reflections from the experiences of others (including those of the mentee), executive or other education courses, or books that illustrate key aspects important for the mentee (and potentially the mentor). The constant willingness to learn is a key aspect of a mentor; it provides not only credibility within the environment of their own organization, but also shows the importance of self-renewal, and being able to provide additional insights to mentees as they themselves supplement their own educations. Indeed, it also provides a mechanism by which the mentee and the mentor can challenge one another to learn and discuss, side-by-side, concepts that are important to both from different perspectives. This approach can be extraordinarily valuable from both a learning perspective of the mentee, where new concepts can be seen in the light of a mentor with more experience and a view that adds color that might be quite enlightening, and to the mentor, where he or she becomes exposed to novel concepts of which they would have otherwise not been aware.

"A wise teacher learns in the midst of teaching; a wise student teaches in the midst of learning".

-Mollie Marti

THE NEED FOR MULTIPLE MENTORS

In virtually every position, the types of skills and requirements are myriad and encompass a number of different interacting components that is truly individual. As example, if in a research department in a company understanding what is required to have one's research move to the next stage may be as important as understanding the politics to get onto the review agenda; if in academia, the need for senior collaborators to help with grants from specific agencies may be important, as well as how to negotiate more "protected" time for research outside of administrative duties. These examples indicate that the experiences needed to support one's goals and objectives almost certainly will span a whole host of different individuals, thus requiring more than a single mentor who can address all aspects of development. While it is both appropriate and wise to seek out an individual to act as mentor, preparation is the best first action. Understanding the types of skills one requires to advance does engender a necessary initial step and need to be self-reflective, and focus upon those skills where a mentoring relationship could be helpful. This extends to different parts of one's career or life situations as well; with such evolution, comes the need to add additional mentors who can help address the new set of challenges being faced. Interestingly, there is also the idea that the addition of mentors can not only be a more formal process, asking for an individual to serve as a mentor, but also an observational one; watching a person whom is admired and/or trusted, and understanding how she or he acts in given situations that can be emulated is also a form of being mentored. This less direct form provides no feedback *per se*, but provides potential lessons from afar. However, given the opportunity, a more interactive approach can be even more valuable. In my own experience, I had one person who acted not only as an informal mentor, but a formal one as well; I tried to observe his actions in different scenarios, and at the same time had regular interactions with him in a mentoring relationship. Years later, he and I still occasionally talk, although he is now retired, but nonetheless I will oftentimes think about how he might act in a given situation that we either shared in the past or at least discussed. This past mentorship relationship, combined with mentor relationships I have currently, provides a richness in experience that advises me within situations in common discussed with several mentors, and provides another perspective in ones I have discussed only with a single mentor. Hence, having multiple mentors (both formal and informal/observational) can be very beneficial in development, and is almost certain to be helpful as professional and personal circumstances change.

FINDING A MENTOR

It is mildly surprising to note that many technical executives or executives-to-be with whom I have been associated have never had a mentoring relationship, or define it as a supervisor–employee one. This might be somewhat expected, as our initial academic relationships might qualify as such, but perhaps as articulated in earlier chapters these are not the ideal relationships to emulate. Nonetheless, while technical expertise is indeed something that requisite skills may require additional guidance, the burgeoning executive will find other areas as well, and perhaps more importantly, that require a mentorship relationship. Often this revolves around the new responsibilities engendered by the position, or areas that might have been a part of the job in the past, now have become more prominent. Hence, when looking for appropriate mentors, one must be willing to look beyond just the technical department or even the larger division in which one resides; in fact, it may be outside of R&D in general, or even one's own institution. As noted, after providing yourself some insight into the skills needed to fulfill goals, think broadly about who might be able to help you with these items. Often, these are people that are already either well known to you, or individuals that you may have seen and admired. Clearly, those who are close in proximity have the additional advantage to potentially be more accessible, although certainly in good mentorship relationships, especially today with Skype and other modes of facile communication, even longer distance relationships can exist (*e.g.* Indian Institute of Technology Mentorship Programme; see sidebar). Indeed, I have had mentorship relationships with individuals on the opposite coast, where frequent communication by email/phone, with occasional in-person meetings when in the same town, was very fulfilling.

One particular issue I have noted in some mentorship relationships, especially in ones with R&D personnel, is the hesitancy of *asking* for such a relationship. A former colleague – who was already at the director level – once asked me quite bluntly, "How do you *get* a mentor?" After having discussions with individuals such as this colleague and others, it is clear that the fear of rejection creates much of the hesitancy, as well as the embarrassment of asking for assistance. The ironic aspect is that most experienced leaders – the ones who might be excellent choices for a mentor – are actually quite used to being one. Of course, while there are those who might not desire such a relationship (see above), even in that context you can learn what *not* to do as well when mentoring others (see below). But what I have found is that getting together with a potential mentor, whether over coffee or a meal, and letting them know that you admire their skills and judgment, and the impact they have already had on you, noting that you would like to learn from them, is an excellent way to approach the subject. Ask if they would be willing to answer questions from you, and take time to discuss specific areas. My experience is it is the exception that the potential mentor does not accept the relationship; indeed, just by asking creates a strong bond – you are telling someone that you admire them, and

TABLE 11.1 The Process of Finding a Mentor

Self-reflect: identify areas of development
Search broadly for those who might be able to act as mentor; look both inside and outside of the department/division
Think about both formal and informal mentorship in your search
Initiate the dialogue if a formal mentorship relationship
Follow up: create regular interactions

want to learn from them. It is a significant compliment. Table 11.1 summarizes the process.

It is important not only to find a mentor, but to continue to nurture the relationship. Regular meetings with specific questions and/or subjects are key, and the willingness not only to be inquisitive, but to provide subject matter – ideas, books, articles, or other vehicles to learn and discuss. While open ended conversations can have value, remember that the mentor is often quite busy, and the interactions should best be at least somewhat focused; this provides not only value to the mentee and the gradual acquisition of knowledge, but also further strengthens the relationship. Without question, even though it is implicit, continuing to express gratitude is important, to both highlight the value of the relationship to you as well as to ensure that the mentor both understands this and wishes to continue the relationship. This is true for both mentors with whom you have had a long-term relationship, as well as new ones where the relationship is just beginning.

THE IMPORTANCE OF MENTORING OTHERS

"It's bad enough in life to do without something YOU want; but confound it, what gets my goat is not being able to give somebody something you want THEM to have".

-Truman Capote

While finding mentors is an important aspect of managing oneself, almost equally important is the need to mentor others who might have either less experience or want to gain insight into areas that the technical executive has already within their armamentarium. This is an important way not only to increase one's skills as a manager, but also a significant growth opportunity, as reflecting on past experiences in a way that is helpful to others can help clarify your own, as well as potential for acquisition of new knowledge and relationships. Moreover, such self-reflection often hardens the lessons learned and acts as a reminder of how your own experiences have shaped you, and how you might be able to help others – particularly in those times when your own actions might not have resulted in the best outcomes, and providing advice can at least help others avoid potential similar ones. Indeed, reliving any negative experience when used to help another can be quite therapeutic, and provide the satisfaction that your advice can help avoid the negative consequences of less than stellar judgment (at least at the time).

Like the expectations of being a mentee, being a mentor should be considered a commitment with the requisite time and effort. Those who come to you asking for help are doing so, as noted earlier, because they admire your abilities; we owe such individuals our very best in order to ensure that this generation continues to improve, as we hope our own continues to do so; there is no exception to the rule that to succeed, there always has to be someone else who has helped along the way, even if that person is not specifically known. In this vein, it is necessary to have in the forefront of mind that the mentorship relationship is about the mentee – the focus needs to be on the needs of the individual seeking guidance. While it is clear that exchange of ideas can result in changing of focus between the mentor and mentee, it should always revert back to the latter; our obligation as a mentor is to ensure that the mentees are gaining from the experience. This does not imply that constructive feedback should be avoided; in fact, this is a key aspect of any mentorship relationship; however, negative criticism is usually not helpful, although positive guidance is. Often it is better to go through various scenarios and examples with the individual regarding actions or ideas, bringing in one's own experience, as a teaching methodology. But also recall that this is not a tutelage, but rather a mentor relationship; avoiding the perception of the all-knowing teacher and the student vessel is paramount. By doing this your experiences will resonate more fully, and help the mentee potentially see other ways of handling similar (often difficult) situations. And, by being enthusiastic and positive about the abilities and potential of mentees, and by creating a supportive space, the mentor and mentee will both benefit.

Finally, understand that you will/should not be the only mentor for any individual who asks for mentorship. It is both appropriate and reasonable to refer mentees to others who might have additional skills that the technical executive mentor feels would be beneficial to the mentee in his or her quest for personal and professional growth. Such relationships should be encouraged in order to fulfill your role as a mentor – viz. recognizing additional experiences helpful for the mentee on their development journey. Similarly, at some point, whether at a career transition, changes in geography, movement in different direction personally or professionally, fulfillment of the objectives of the relationship, or other reasons, the mentorship relationship will begin to wind down. Hopefully, the reason for winding down will not be because of atrophy from a suboptimal relationship, but because tangible growth and expansion has occurred with the mentee, and that the need for regular interaction has become less necessary as a result. While the relationship often is never severed, the activity does become less, although the learnings are in place lifelong. Moreover, in good mentoring relationships, becoming true peers creates a new and fulfilling relationship that enhances both the former mentor and mentee in the way that is unique and positive for both parties. In my own experience, from those whom have been mentees, either as students, post-docs, managers, or even most recently other

CEOs, I have found huge satisfaction at seeing them advance and succeed. One former engineer, who I was privileged to mentor as a CEO, wrote me a note of thanks when he himself became a CEO, stating, "I have always kept in my mind your advice, 'Know what you want to be when you grow up'; here I am today, thanks to you". As a mentor, these are gifts of unspeakable value, and without question, help you get through some of the most challenging days.

"The excellence of a gift lies in its appropriateness rather than in its value".

-Charles Dudley Warner

REFERENCES

Eisenberg, M., 2011. The Physician Scientist's Career Guide. Springer, New York.

Sanders, T., 2002. Love is the Killer App. Three Rivers Press, New York.

Wooden, J., Tobin, J., 2002. They Call Me Coach. McGraw-Hill, New York.

Project Perspectives

"The trick to forgetting the big picture is to look at everything close up".

-Chuck Palahniuk

"We often need to lose sight of our priorities in order to see them".

-John Irving

"The greatest risk to man is not that he aims too high and misses, but that he aims too low and hits".

-Michaelangelo

Widening a View Brian had been a scientist at the company for many years, working in the Discovery part of the organization, rising to the position of senior scientist. He had done considerable work in the area of second messenger systems in cells, and was considered both inside and outside of the organization an expert in the field. He supported several early stage teams, mostly with scientists who facilitated experiments with compounds that had as a potential mechanism of action such second messengers; his group acted to confirm through screening the validity of the mechanistic assumption. The assays developed in Brian's group were indeed impressive, and most believed within research that these provided the firm with a level of competitive advantage. With changes in management, however, while acknowledging the expertise within all of research, the company's senior management decided to put into the early stage teams clinical development representatives, in order to provide input and assess the programs at that stage. They were to help determine both clinical viability and matching of the target product profile of the various projects that were ongoing, as part of the corporate pathway initiative giving guidance to even the Discovery and Research groups. Brian personally bristled at having these people present on "his" teams, and several times dismissed any clinical person from team meetings that he occasionally attended. This prompted a call from the just hired

VP of R&D supervising Brian, noting the importance of this initiative, and the emphasis of the CEO on the need for all to be aware of the importance of a development thought process throughout the division. Brian was incensed; why the need for Research and Discovery to have to deal with clinical issues?

IT'S A BUSINESS PROJECT, NOT JUST A RESEARCH PROJECT

One trap that can be very easy to fall into as an R&D director or staff is a myopic view of one's work; this is understandable, as much of the time the level of sophistication within which we toil is significant, and is challenging even to explain to the well initiated. We get our experiments done, and view and interpret this new knowledge, determining and assessing either success or failure of our respective hypotheses. I am sure that most if not all of us have experienced being lost in the data, having to assess different possibilities, and then emerging with what we believe to be the correct interpretation in order to go to the next step.

The challenge with this is that we become insulated from the rest of the organization when this occurs. It is not that we mean to generate the data in a vacuum, or that there is any intention not to communicate; it is that the nature of R&D can be that the experiments being performed can take on a life of their own, particularly if they are complex and need some level of knowledge base to determine if a specific endpoint has been reached. It may take weeks to comprehend the data. Nonetheless, this often puts us in a silo, where our inputs and outputs are within the (highly) technical realm, and further communication is not performed – either because of a lack of perceived need, or often, because it is thought, "someone else will do it". Neither situation is optimal, and further isolates us from the rest of the organization, becoming an "ivory tower" within the firm.

As we move toward management, it is clear that we need to be cognizant of the larger picture, *viz.* of the organization and stakeholders in particular. Assuming we are employed by a firm that has as one of its goals to create value, we need to understand that research, manifest as Discovery such as in Brian's group, cannot be considered in isolation from the goals and objectives to the rest of the firm. While it might be argued that the experiments being performed at this level are too early for true consideration around clinical (or other) issues, this could not be farther from the truth. There are always opportunity costs associated with any activity that expends resources with the firm, whether that is in R&D or marketing; choosing *what* to do is directly related to *what to spend*. While Brian's group was clearly world class, whether they should be testing every compound or any compound should be part of the assessment process in order to determine whether this was the best use of resources. Having the clinical group be part of the team was an excellent start for trying to understand better what types of things were being done early on in R&D; rather than be resistant to this effort, it might have been better if Brian had embraced it, as it could have helped him set priorities for his own group. As technical executives, we need to understand the goals of the firm in order to best determine the types of opportunities that are within our groups. Despite the unique circumstances around R&D, as a knowledge genera-tion business we are obligated to break down barriers, rather than fortify them.

"Historically communications have been stuck in a bunch of different silos".

-Brad Garlinghouse

As responsibilities broaden in the role as technical executive, it often becomes apparent the need to seek alignment from a more diverse group than previously. We need to best understand the impact of the programs on other divisions, as well as how they align with corporate objectives. I can recall an instance where surreptitiously we discovered by chance a novel binding of a molecule on a recep-tor that had to do with an uncommon disease; we initially pursued this mecha-nism, virtually to the point of missing on some other objectives that needed to be accomplished in our well-established therapeutic area. When describing this to the research leadership, they rightly pointed out that this was not within our area currently, and that it was thus not aligned with the current strategy of the company despite being interesting on a scientific basis. It is important that we are able to see the larger picture as we move further into our management role, since it is clear that there are less degrees of freedom than in our own labs or even groups. While at times it may be appropriate to move down a pathway in an entrepreneurial way, we should do this with a keen sense of value creation vis-à-vis risk evaluation given what the other parts of the organization are both aligned toward and need from our respective groups. Figure 12.1 shows a schematic reflecting these ideas.

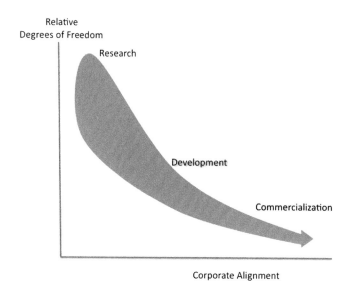

FIGURE 12.1   Relative degrees of freedom *v.* corporate alignment. While there is an increase in flexibility at the level of R&D, it is neither infinite, nor is the need for corporate alignment zero; moving through the value chain towards commercialization requires an increased emphasis on alignment with limited degrees of freedom.

Finally, as technical executives we need to be mindful of the need for operating excellence within the R&D function. Again, while our function is to generate knowledge, and thus is unique within the firm as an area that can be difficult to quantify with numbers, the ability to at least quantify the *why* and the *how* becomes important as we justify our efforts within the broader organization. Oftentimes as noted R&D can be accused of "paralysis by analysis"; such issues resonate with those who have a more diverse background as well as scientists who understand risk and uncertainty. As the depth of the role we play in the organization expands, we need to be able to identify and create *actionable* knowledge that will have high priority for the consideration within and outside of the R&D function consistent with corporate objectives. Framing operations in this way does allow both a better comparability to other parts of the firm, as well as clarifying the contribution to the rest of the firm in a more tangible manner. While this may not be possible for every aspect of R&D, our efforts should be sufficient in order to at least demonstrate our attention to this area, as much as other executives dedicate to their respective areas.

"A company can seize extra-ordinary opportunities only if it is very good at the ordinary operations".

-Marcel Telles

DEVELOPMENT OF PIPELINE

With that noted, with the concept of alignment, particularly in more mature organizations, as technical executives we need to be aware of the pipeline to be generated within our departments and divisions. This too needs to be in the context of the broader organization; most of the time this is part of the portfolio management process (see Chapter 5), with respect to the products both in development, in the market, and with respect to the latter, at specific parts of the product life cycle. As a junior executive, my concept of a portfolio reflected my inexperience; I believed it was just that we had ongoing projects within the R&D part of the organization that would be moving ahead based on data. It was more structured around a perceived lynchpin of research, where the process of product development, in my mind, truly began. While certainly many laboratory directors and staff would find this assessment hopelessly naïve, the reality is that many of us spoke of the pipeline in this manner (perhaps reflecting our origins in academia?). Nonetheless, there are a variety of concepts of which to take account when discussing the pipeline of the organization. While potentially obvious, it is clear that program risk is part and parcel of this consideration, particularly when tackling new areas of product development that require either paradigm shifts or are truly disruptive (see Chapter 6 for discussion on disruptive innovations). Not only is adoption a potential challenge, but just moving to the next stage of development might be a significant hurdle. As extension, the stage of the program is a corollary to risk; for most products, the risk and uncertainty can decline when a program has moved forward, and should be considered when thinking about a pipeline of products/opportunities for the organization. In that context, it should be mentioned that within the development of a pipeline, there can be non-product aspects thereof, which reflect corporate priorities related to needs of different parts of the organization; examples could be an update of a manufacturing plant, or hiring more marketing personnel because of an upcoming launch. These are part of the portfolio as they reflect resource allocation, and despite the fact that they are not product related *per se*, they encompass areas that need to be addressed by the firm. Other aspects of the pipeline to be considered include the relative maturity of products already in the marketplace – are they new products just launched, or have they reached maturity in their product life cycle? Are life cycle management approaches appropriate to start to be developed either as new uses, modifications, or repositioning? These may impact both on pipeline expenditures, and as well, on R&D expenditures to support such areas. A consideration may also be to either reflect or use business development activities in the pipeline; there may have been activity bringing products into the firm that need support at any part of the R&D value chain, or require resources for commercial needs; this also is part of the portfolio process. In the end, the construction of the portfolio really reflects the nature of the organization to create the most value possible with its resources. Both the development and the discovery and research parts of the firm need to be integrated into this thought process, and technical executives ought to be cognizant of how not only the programs within R&D fit, but also the other aspects to ensure consistent value creation of the organization. Table 12.1 summarizes these aspects.

Interestingly, a key realization when moving into a technical executive position was the view that innovation did not belong only in R&D, but occurred all over the organization, including in processes, commercial approaches, and/or financial engineering (legal, of course), but it was also something that

TABLE 12.1 Pipeline Construction

Consideration	Example
Program Risk	Novelty of program *v.* Sustaining Innovation
Timing of Programs	Stage of project; early *v.* late
Corporate Priorities	Costs of manufacturing plant (*viz.* opportunity cost considerations)
Market Maturity	Life cycle management of mature product *v.* New product just launched into market
External Programs	Use of Business Development to supplement pipeline in Product Development Stage; New product brought into organization

as a larger firm we had the benefit of looking outward as well for innovations. I had grown up in the R&D part of the organization, and had a somewhat arrogant view that the innovations we were either developing or had developed were the best out in the industry, and that others were of lesser quality if not originating from inside the firm. Just like the epiphany of innovations outside of the technical group, the understanding that there were technologies that could fit inside the firm from outside the company – whether in research, development, the commercial parts of the organization, or elsewhere – was something that I came to realize reflected my need for broader acceptance. The company needs to utilize *any* technology that the organization's resources could access in order to create value for shareholders. We all have the natural pride of ownership of our specific programs and projects; however, we need to be well aware that within our own pipeline management process, we may either find a hole or a need to supplement to ensure a regular output of products or programs that customers believe have utility exist. Without question I have been at firms that while understanding these concepts, put very high barriers to entry on programs to be brought into the firm (much higher than we placed on our own programs) because of a subconscious bias. As technical executives, we have a responsibility to the organization to be wary of this mindset, which might not be popular (at least initially) as these may compete with our own programs. However, in consideration of the discussion around pipeline, finding the right set of assets to create the most value should be the penultimate goal, whether this includes internally developed ones or those that can be obtained from external sources.

Not Invented Here

The "not invented here" syndrome is a common one particularly in high technology organizations; these kinds of companies usually have been founded and successful based on their abilities to develop and commercialize cutting-edge technology. It has been noted, interestingly enough, that larger companies suffer this to a significantly larger extent than smaller ones; indeed, these companies tend to utilize the same innovations to derive programs and projects for an extended period compared to smaller firms (deemed "creative myopia" by Agrawal et al). Also not unsurprising is the data that the closer a potentially acquired technology is to one within a firm (*viz.* from a competing company) the more resistance encountered within the firm, *even if that technology is demonstrably better*. Further, it is successful companies that most sustain the not invented here syndrome; this seems to be industry independent, from manufacturing to software. Nonetheless, it has been found that even in the academic setting, the not invented here syndrome does apply, extending this phenomenon outside of the industrial setting. Finally, there seems to be a decreased barrier to entry of technologies into firms when considering *open* innovation models; by adopting a "network" approach, there is at least a mitigation of risk of one's own technology, allowing presumed increased innovation capacity and performance with respect to integration into the firm's

Not Invented Here—cont'd
programs or projects without "abandoning" one's own technology. Hence, the not invented here syndrome exists in diverse settings including both industry and academia; by use of an open innovation model, there is at least the potential to diminish the perceived risk (both internal and external) of bringing in technology into a given organization.

Kathoefer DG, Leker J. Knowledge transfer in academia: an exploratory study on the Not-Invented-Here Syndrome. Journal of Technology Transfer 37:658–75, 2012;

Hussinger K, Wastyn A. In Search for the Not-Invented-Here Syndrome: The Role of Knowledge Sources and Firm Success. Center for European Economics Research, Discussion Paper No. 11-048, 2011;

Agarwal A, Cockburn I, Rosell C. Not Invented Here? Innovation in company towns. Journal of Urban Economics 67: 78–89, 2010.

RELATIONSHIPS

As has been mentioned in earlier chapters (*e.g.* Chapter 9), creating relationships outside of one's own department or group is a fundamental aspect of the technical executive when moving up the management track; these become new peers with whom one will be associated for the broader objectives within the areas of responsibility. Certainly, it is self-evident that such relationships can create an improved level of cooperation between technical areas and others, particularly those that do not commonly interface or have similar backgrounds. However, there is great utility in not only reaching out to others within the organization, but also encouraging staff within your area of responsibility to do so as well. One thing I was surprised to discover when moving into the management track was the feeling of fear that non-technical personnel sometimes express when it comes to the scientific areas within their own organizations; there is both articulated and non-articulated intimidation noted about the science and/or engineering when speaking with individuals not trained technically but who were otherwise very smart and accomplished. Conversely, and not unsurprisingly, technical staff also felt the same intimidation when discussing areas outside of their expertise – finance, accounting, marketing, sales, human resources, law *etc.* oftentimes struck fear into the hearts of our respective groups as well. Bringing together technical staff with others from diverse areas in the organization can diminish this mutual intimidation considerably, particularly if done in an informal and non-threatening way. Moreover, encouraging our own groups to work with their peers to understand their areas better can be a significantly beneficial exercise, and have considerable benefits for the organization as a whole. While the team structure of most firms can accomplish this to a certain extent, a bit more delving into an area with individual team members can yield dividends outside of the particular program with whom each is a member; it can create a lasting perspective on the needs and pressures from these other groups outside of R&D that can help when serving on other teams or task forces.

> **"Clockspeed"**
>
> Charles Fine used this term in his book when describing the temporary advantages for most industries due to the rapid changes occurring almost on a daily basis. As an interesting comparison, he utilized concepts from biology – evolutionary, phenotypic, and molecular – to describe the processes in business, from survival of the fittest in the context of adaption to the marketplace, to cloning as related to building capabilities in engineering. The interface between the various parts of the firm to create adaptability is a key aspect within the ability to manage clockspeed, as noted from various examples in diverse industries, from photographic film to servers to bicycles. Being able to coordinate different functions within the firm as well as define the manufacturing and supply chain(s) are key in order to sustain competitive advantage. Moreover, developing an extended enterprise has particular influence on the system dynamics of product development; indeed, competitive advantage can emerge from being able to develop and design the product, process, and supply chain *simultaneously*. This obviously has key ramifications on the relationships within the firm, and the need for obvious cooperation and synergy between the research, development, commercial, manufacturing, and corporate groups, at a minimum, in order to best sustain the earliest and most enduring advantage. Hence, ensuring relationships and value chain transparency across the organization has important consequences not only for working relationships but also for the ability to maximize the chances of competitive advantage.
>
> *Fine CH. Clockspeed: Winning Industry Control in the Age of Temporary Advantage. Cambridge, Perseus, 1998.*

ABSORPTIVE CAPACITY

When leading a clinical group I was introduced to the concept of "absorptive capacity"; we were putting in place new processes and procedures in order to inculcate as well as distribute new learnings. My supervisor at the time, who preceded me at the company by about seven months, introduced the term to me when discussing how the organization would be able to accept these initiatives. Absorptive capacity refers to the ability not only to identify and absorb new information, but apply it to value-creating means often applicable *throughout* the organization. Being able to *distribute* knowledge and learnings within the firm along with implementation of particular practices is specific within absorbtive capacity. It has clear strategic significance, and integrates different aspects within the firm, including the inherent knowledge within the organization, with external connections where influential knowledge resides (*e.g.* universities, other firms in the space, the extended enterprise *etc.*). The relatedness of this inherent knowledge inside the organization to the new knowledge to absorb provides a basis by which such latter information could be diffused and integrated. There is also specific evidence that technical managers play a key role in absorptive capacity, whether as a requisite internal source, or identification of from alternative sources of knowledge within the organization, such as either previous adopters of similar processes, prior events, and/or complementary practices. We as technical executives influence the adoption decisions, and thus have to be concerned about ensuring that *access* is available to those who have had previous experience and have adopted the processes for our respective groups. This allows the dissemination of information by exposure to others, further enhancing the adoptive capability within the firm.

This concept was important in looking more broadly on how our group/ division would be able to integrate some of the new initiatives being brought in by my supervisor and me to improve the processes that were currently lacking within the organization. By identifying the current inherent knowledge base of the specific units we were interested in updating, we could decipher important *related* processes that had been adapted and implemented, as well as those who had been instrumental in those efforts. The data is pretty clear that just providing information to staff on new (even related) processes and expecting lasting implementation is unrealistic; some prior experience is necessary to ensure uptake. By utilizing those individuals who had been part of a successful assimilation of novel processes/tasks related to our efforts, we were able to work together in a collaborative way to best propagate and distribute these new capabilities within the group (and have them stick).

Absorptive Capacity: Underdeveloped Nations

In addition to firms in the industrial sector, it is clear that countries also have absorptive capacity. Indeed, the development of technological and innovative capabilities is directly related to economic growth in such countries. However, in certain parts of the world, there has been less robust accumulation of these capabilities despite global assistance from other countries. This is a particularly challenging aspect as the ability to create self-sustaining industries and an economic base is relevant to maintain (or initiate) the development of the country. Indeed, even foreign direct investment (*via* international companies) or promoting university and local industry relationships has been at best only minimally successful; it has been suggested and demonstrated that this is due to a limitation of absorptive capacity within the country. Recent data suggests that "intermediaries" might be able to play a role in helping smaller organizations to increase their absorptive capacity, by interpreting and translating the information from more sophisticated sources that the emerging country company needs in order to facilitate diffusion of knowledge relevant to these entities. NGOs play an important role in this, as purveyors of potential experience and being accessible by local companies to create lasting knowledge accumulation and process development. Indeed, being able to utilize diverse knowledge bases such as local universities as well as international companies also enhances the relationship between those organizations that are

Continued

Absorptive Capacity: Underdeveloped Nations—cont'd

relatively local to the domestic firms developing such capacity. Hence, by NGOs acting as an accessible resource, transfer of knowledge to local companies can increase their absorptive capacity, similar to that noted within industrial firms.

Szogs A, Chaminade C, Azatyan R. Building absorptive capacity in less developed countries: The case of Tanzania. Working Paper 2008/05, Centre for Innovation, Research and Competence in the Learning Economy (CIRCLE), Lund University.

REFERENCES

Cohen, W.M., Levinthal, D.A., 1990. Absorptive Capacity: A New Perspective on Learning and Innovation. Administrative Science Quarterly 35, 128–152.

Glen, P., 2003. Leading Geeks. How To Manage and Lead People Who Deliver Technology. Jossey-Bass, New York.

Joyce, W., Nohria, N., Roberson, B., 2003. What Really Works: The 4+2 Formula for Sustained Business Success. HarperBusiness, New York.

Lenox, M., King, A., 2004. Prospects for Developing Absorptive Capacity Through Internal Information Provision. Strategic Management Journal 25, 331–345.

Managing Upward

"He who cannot follow cannot lead".

-Benjamin Franklin

"The person of knowledge has always been expected to take responsibility for being understood. It is barbarian arrogance to assume that the layman can or should make the effort to understand the specialist".

-Peter Drucker

"Men who do things without being told draw the most wages".

-Edwin H. Stuart

Knowing Your Audience Mary had been a medical virologist when she had entered into the biotech industry, and been involved in several programs that had reached late stage development, although none of the products had been approved for marketing authorization by regulatory authorities. Nonetheless, she was excellent at ensuring that all of the senior managers at her early stage company were well aware of both each step and the results of the programs with which she was charged, and spent considerable time simplifying study results and leaving messages on their voicemails. In addition, she was able to provide summaries to her supervisor, which had slightly more detail than her voicemails, and provided updates on team interactions particularly outside of the clinical development group. She never shied away from difficult decisions, but consistently provided presentations outlining alternatives, pros and cons of each, and a suggested decision, based on the available evidence, and the assumptions associated with each. She was thoughtful in approach, and almost never negative in demeanor in public forums, and even if disagreeing with a point, she could do so without being disagreeable. Mary had been promoted from being a team leader to director before she moved companies to become the Vice President of Clinical

Development at a larger pharmaceutical company. Within that role, she con-
tinued to be highly communicative; however, the CEO, also a former clinical
development executive, asked her to stop providing him the voicemails she had
done in the past, and instead report to her supervisor the more detailed results.
In turn, her supervisor (the Senior Vice President of Development) asked that
she continue the updates, but focus on a needs assessment within her depart-
ment and report on this regularly. Moreover, she was told to include the Human
Resource Representative in her regular updates, and not the Global Head of
Sales and Marketing. Mary altered her actions as requested, but could not help
asking herself, "Why the different approach?".

FIRST, UNDERSTAND

Any type of interpersonal interaction, both professional and personal, is always
nuanced with subtleties based on the players involved. This extends to the ways
we adapt to everything from our episodic interactions with baristas from the
local coffee shops to our spouses; we put in efforts as appropriate in order to
facilitate the communication and relationship based on the context (assuredly
much more in the latter than the former!). It is obviously no different when
involved in an organization where we have supervisors; in particular, we must
learn and adjust to effectively work with others, and as well, understand what
is expected of us and how we are to be evaluated and perceived. The complexity of human behavior and interpretation significantly influences these aspects.
Hence, it is important not only to understand how our supervisors "tick", but
also to be able to communicate our own perceptions of the working relationship,
adapting it to the supervisor's own style.

As example, the manner of communication is often important, based on
whether the manager is an introvert or an extrovert; Peter Drucker has described
this in roughly equivalent terms of "readers" and "listeners". The extrovert or
listener tends to talk to understand, while the reader or introvert often prefers
to read initially before discussion; obviously, these are addressed differently.
Indeed, this can be a manifestation of the style of working that managers might
have, which has value for interpreting the actions and/or consequences in
response to circumstances. Indeed, while there are many personality inventories
that have been used in different organizations, regardless of the system, it is a
valuable skill to be able to ascertain the personality type of our supervisors in
order to better work with them in the professional context. A convenient (but
again, by no means only) one that has been used in various settings that is fairly
easily learnt is the Myers Briggs Type Indicator; it is based on the psychological theories of Carl Jung, and focuses on normal populations, and in particular,
the natural differences and preferences individuals may tend toward, based on
certain *dichotomies*. These dichotomies are the preferences that describe the
Myers Briggs "Type" into which a person falls; again, these are personality preferences, which helps understand behavior (see Table 13.1 for a more
complete elaboration). The four descriptive dichotomies include: introversion

TABLE 13.1 Myers Briggs Type Indicator Dichotomies and Traits

Attitudes

Extraversion: Draw stimulation and energy from interaction with others; have a distinct need to "be heard"; prefer to work with others to generate ideas; "think out loud" most of the time	Introversion: Draw stimulation and energy from being alone and/or having time to oneself; tend to want to prepare for meetings (and expect others to do the same); like to work alone initially to generate ideas

Perceiving Function

Sensing: Prefer precision; very organized; often satisfied with the status quo; thorough and detail oriented; like to see tangible results and task oriented	Intuitive: Concept oriented; interested in overlaps and looking for connectedness; more general than precise; often looking for how things could be different than what exists currently

Judging Function

Thinking: Objective; believe decisions should be made on evidence at hand than other considerations such as emotional overtones; better to be right on an issue than liked; tend toward logic and scientific proof	Feeling: Believe considerations of the feelings of others should always be taken into account; accommodating, often to a fault; are less interested in hard evidence than having harmony in decision making; avoid interpersonal conflict as much as possible

Lifestyle

Judging: Don't appreciate surprises; believe "a place for everything and everything in its place"; prefer to work tasks to completion to get them out of the way (even if known of the possibility of repeating aspects); make many lists and will add items completed just to cross them off	Perceiving: Avoid order; easily distracted and spontaneous; often been called a procrastinator; tend not to plan but to react to tasks and situations

v. extraversion ("attitudes"), sensing v. intuition ("perceiving" function), thinking v. feeling ("judging" function), and judging v. perception ("lifestyle"). By understanding the preferred dichotomies of a given individual, as well as our own, we can better find ways to match working styles (or *potentially* anticipate behaviors). To be clear, though, these and other instruments can be helpful in describing personality preferences, but are not intended for detection of abilities or prediction of job performance. Nonetheless, making an effort to at least understand the personality of one's supervisor – and one's own personality – can be of value to best adapt to the potential synergies (or avoid potential conflicts) that our personality preferences might entail. There are some excellent texts that provide helpful hints on using these Type Indicators, as well as the lay assessment of potential Types without the formal inventory questionnaire. While Mary did indeed communicate well, she probably needed to take into account the different ways her new supervisor – and the CEO – wanted to be updated in her activities; while her initial approach worked for her old company, she had not adequately made the effort to understand better the personalities of her new one, and how they worked. Proactively evaluating the working styles of the other senior managers at Mary's new firm would have been wise before embarking upon her *own* usual style of work.

Another key component is a firm comprehension of not only one's own stresses and goals, but the ones that are facing our supervisors. To be effective, we need to best understand where the key pressures are for our bosses, and also how they relate to his or her *milieu*. This is the basis on how we get our job done – by obtaining the resources necessary to alleviate the issues facing our respective departments, manifest by addressing the overlapping interests between our supervisor's goals and our own. This certainly encompasses the need for clear communication and understanding of roles and responsibilities between supervisor and report. As has been noted previously, a good manager will provide clear guidance on expectations; and a good report, like a good manager, will discuss proactively the 4Ps (see Chapter 10), *integrating* the understanding of the supervisor goals and objectives. Hence, being able to concisely discuss the projects and programs, as well as how the manager is doing – acquiring information on what areas of stress they are under – and reporting on one's own perception of the department is a very cooperative way to work with one's supervisor toward shared goals. Indeed, even the question regarding how the report can do better does provide an open ended opportunity to discuss perceptions on performance and expectations. The 4Ps can thus help not only within the context of our direct reports, but also when engaging with our supervisors to provide information and obtain feedback necessary for our jobs.

One very key component of understanding is the time constraints most senior managers face on a day-to-day basis; unfortunately, this very aspect can result in some severe misunderstandings between the supervisor and the report. I know that I have at times believed my supervisor was ignoring or even being passive aggressive when I provided him a detailed report that he noted he needed "right away", having dropped everything and worked through the night to provide him. Despite leaving messages asking if he needed anything more, I received no response, which was unusual for him. My imagination was running wild on my missing something or providing an inadequate summary when he got back to me that he had received the material, but had been in high pressure meetings and had not had time to respond. Indeed, I myself try to avoid this when I ask reports for vital information requiring significant effort, but I have failed to acknowledge receipt at times and must apologize profusely subsequently (which usually involves a lunch or a beer). If the relationship has been adequately developed between supervisor and report, most of the time these issues will not be significant, although each party needs to be sensitive to it; we must understand that time is the most valuable thing we as technical executives have. I know that in all the discussions I have had with other executives in industries as diverse as oil exploration to oceanography, the lack of time is the universal complaint in all of their lives. Hence, as a resource, we need to be respectful of our supervisor's time, and understand that the compression can at times create suboptimal situations that are unavoidable. But having a clear and communicative relationship with our supervisors, understanding how they work, goes a long way to minimize anxiety on either side.

Finally, especially in new jobs or companies, understanding the working environment is important. This addresses both the supervising manager and the report, and hence, it is important in the context of the company *environs* within which the organization exists. A convenient way to consider this is through the paradigm of "organizational lenses" (see References). Making the effort to understand the mechanical systems ("strategic" organizational lens), the social systems ("political" organizational lens), and the value systems ("cultural" organizational lens) can yield important perspectives of the supervisor who needs to reflect such in their own goals. In the strategic lens, the organization is goal-directed, where the organization is designed to achieve agreed upon goals; the political lens notes the importance of power and influence, where organizations reflect the outcomes of contests for power of internal stakeholders; and finally, the cultural lens is based around values and assumptions and mores of entrenched mental maps typically organically grown. Viewing the organization with these (and other) lenses can provide valuable inputs on how different managers might interpret organizational goals, which may well give different conclusions but should be considered carefully, as your supervisor may only look at the organization in one way. While there is no "right" way to view the organizational environment, the key is to recognize the importance of these diverse views on both the supervisor and the report. Table 13.2 delineates some of the components of these lenses.

TABLE 13.2 Components of Organizational Lenses

	Strategic Lens	Political Lens	Cultural Lens
System type	Mechanical System	Social System	Values System
Main Theme	Coordination and Control	Competition for Power	Common mental maps, assumptions and characteristics
Goals	Agreed Goals designed by leaders	Contradictory, based on contests	Maintain mores
Leader	Strategist	Coalition Builder	Linked to culture as symbol, shaper or descriptor
Results	Alignment and Fit to Plan	Individual/Group Power	Accomplished through traditions

INITIATIVE

Once, during my travels, I was coming back to the USA from Singapore after a fairly arduous trip; we had had a brutal schedule, little sleep, and as one could imagine, just wanted to get home. I had a connecting flight in Los Angeles, and had to clear customs there. The Border Patrol has a program where "trusted travelers" who had been cleared by the U.S. government could use kiosks at certain entry ports (including Los Angeles) to clear customs, rather than wait in the long lines that typically occurred at such major ports. Upon entry into the hall, I entered into the growing queue at the kiosks, only to find that all three had "gone down". While two border guards stood at the head of the line, appearing not to know what to do, I saw another border guard leave one of the cubicles, come over to us, assess the situation, and direct the now extensive line of increasingly disgruntled passengers into a separate line, where she processed us herself, expeditiously. She did not hesitate to find a solution to a growing problem, which clearly her colleagues had been unable to do. When I spoke with her when it was my turn, I complemented her on her leadership skills; she

A Message to Garcia

In 1899, Elbert Hubbard, the editor and publisher of *The Philistine*, included a small piece called "A Message to Garcia" in the March issue. This was derived from a conversation he had with his son Bert regarding the hero of the Cuban war, and revolved around an individual named Rowan. War had broken out between the United States and Spain, and a message needed to be carried to the leader of the insurgents in Cuba. At the time, no one knew where this leader (General Garcia) was located, except that he was in vast hills of Cuba, behind enemy lines, and there was no mail or telegraph that could reach him. Hubbard describes how Rowan, with only the letter and no direction, "disappeared into the jungle" and after three weeks exited on the other side of the island, having delivered the letter to Garcia. Hubbard goes on to extol the virtues of the man, who did not require explicit direction, instructions, or guidance; he took on the task and promptly went forward to execute. He goes on to note that today we have many Garcias, but we have few Rowans willing to take on an order and accomplish tasks set before them. Hubbard laments the "incapacity for independent action", and uses the standard of "can such a man be entrusted to carry a message to Garcia?" as the penultimate one for employees. While the tone is representative of the time, this has been used to provide example particularly in the military of ways to think about initiative and leadership, and at the time (and since) was/is highly popular. From *The Philistine* "A Message to Garcia" was made into a pamphlet, with requests from numerous military and industrial organizations for reprints. Overall, over 40 million copies were distributed in the United States, Russia, Germany, France, Spain, Turkey, India, China, and Japan.

Hubbard E. A Message to Garcia. *The Philistine, March 1899*, as reported in Project Gutenberg, www.gutenberg.org/ebooks/17195.

was good-natured, and only demurred, noting that "sometimes you just need a little bit of initiative". Indeed, a little bit of initiative goes a long way.

If we understand what the goals and objectives are of our supervisor, we can understand how to use initiative in our own work to complement them. To be able to do the right things without having to be told takes some experience, often obtained with the regular communication as noted with one-on-ones. But being able to facilitate solutions without involving the supervisor, and take on the role of situational leadership, creates a perception of both accomplishment and trust. This is related to the concept as mentioned in earlier chapters around only identifying problems, but not solutions; this is almost the opposite of initiative, in that leaving problems for others to solve may indicate some level of analytical ability, but makes both the group's and the supervisor's jobs harder. Indeed, asking the supervisor to solve problems that we should be able to solve shows a *lack* of initiative, and should create doubt of whether we are the right people for the job. Initiative is thus a trait that supervisors significantly value; it decreases the active management required, and yet results in progress.

SIMPLIFY

As noted previously, the ability to simplify is a specific skill that is highly valued at almost any level within an organization. Especially for technical executives, reporting to one's supervisor the particular messages with respect to technical information or datasets that is accurate but simplified is key; this both saves time and avoids extraneous material that represents a distraction to a given situation. Indeed, I have been on (and learned from) both sides of this issue; when as a junior executive I reported to my supervisor the results of a key experiment in such detail that he asked "Did it work?", to when one of my reports did something similar, concluding his highly detailed and sophisticated presentation with "…significant, at the p<.001 level", which is all I really heard. Of note is that when there *is* a complexity, being able to identify and portray potential alternatives on ways to move forward also clarifies the important issues for efficient decision making. This respects the time of the supervisor and simultaneously enhances the credibility of the report. Understandably then, being clear and concise is markedly appreciated by any supervising manager.

Tactically, it is a derived need within the simplicity paradigm to show understanding of the direction of senior managers. Specifically, we as reports as well as managers should have the appropriate skill of listening carefully (see Chapter 5) – no one likes to have to repeat or re-explain when the counterparty is distracted or not paying attention sufficiently. Wasting time working with reports (or other subordinates) and allowing misunderstanding without prompt clarification is not tolerated by almost any level of executive; as noted, time is every executive's most important resource. Those who can quickly ascertain points being made and actions required – and seek explanation promptly, with the ability to recap concisely – are highly valued in the organization, again, saving time and effort of managers.

Finally, being able to simplify does *not* obviate being precise. There is always a need to be accurate and simultaneously spend the time to think through the data to also be clear and concise. We all must walk a fine line between providing enough detail to ensure what is being presented is understood, but not so much as to overwhelm. Again, proactively constructing our communication strategy is important as we would within any venue (see Chapter 9, Table 9.1).

DELIVER

The organizational reality, and the reason that one needs to understand the goals of the supervisor and his or her working style, is that our job is to make our superiors appear both competent and trustworthy to their superiors. Of course, this is for the overall benefit of the firm, but also to solidify a good working relationship and presumably being noticed as a high potential manager. When considering the more detailed aspects of this component of managing upward, it is clear that one must be able to deliver the goals and objectives that have been tasked, one way or another, to our supervisors through our own work. This entails a clear understanding of such goals and objectives – particularly within the context of being both firmly *defined* and previously discussed. It is never adequate to have excuses, but an especially weak one when failing to deliver is that the task was misunderstood; this engenders a lack of credibility and distrust that can be difficult to overcome. As part of this failure is not being able to successfully achieve the goal either on budget or on time, both of which can have mitigating circumstances, but nonetheless can have bad ramifications if missed, or worse, if it is perceived to have sacrificed one for the other. This suggests the inability to prioritize in order to be successful in the project, creating more active management required by the supervisor.

In the end, this does not make the supervisor look good, and reflects poorly on the report.

"A really great talent finds its happiness in execution".

-Johann Wolfgang von Goethe

CHALLENGING SITUATIONS: THE BAD BOSS

A final note to consider when being cognizant about managing upward is having a supervisor who inhibits their report's abilities to do their jobs, and in turn, creates issues for themselves at the same time. Fundamentally, each situation is different, and there are several approaches to these circumstances, but all begin with clarification and communication, and potentially with a healthy dose of patience. Issues certainly should be approached with a level of sensitivity, reflecting on one's own perception of response if our own reports approached us with the issue, and without question with significant amounts of planning. Whether a supervisor is thought to be distracted, who micromanages, refuses

Five Signs You're a Bad Boss

As managers, we often have blind spots and misperceptions on how we appear to our employees, and can be significantly surprised when we discover these traits unwittingly. One of the most important aspects, then, of being both a better report and supervisor is feedback and communication, and then the willingness to work on the aspects identified that seem to be interfering with the relationship. Diana Middleton's piece in the *Wall Street Journal* identified some signs suggesting you might not be the boss you'd hoped. These are:

Email responses are one word. This can create the perception of curtness with misunderstanding; it suggests that politeness may not be necessary on your part, nor appreciation for the employee.

Little face-to-face interaction. This translates both to using electronic or other non-personal means of communication, which is particularly problematic when needing to have difficult discussions. It also creates the perception of aloofness and inapproachability, with little corresponding trust.

Lots of sick days of employees. Besides the obvious avoidance of a supervisor due to his or her behavior by calling in sick, bad bosses may even *cause* ill health in their respective employees – Middleton quotes a 2008 study in Sweden showing an increase in heart attacks in men who were by self-report poorly managed.

Employees working harder but missing deadlines. Supervisors may become increasingly unreasonable about deadlines when under stress or when new and believing they need "something to prove".

Your emotions are reflected in your voice volume. Screaming at an employee is not only inappropriate to the employee in question, but obviously creates a stressful environment where everyone is on edge, and probably demotivated.

As an employee, seeing this in your supervisor clearly requires some additional investigation on what is causing such behavior, and what needs to be done to try to ameliorate the causes, since it will no doubt affect your productivity. If one sees these signs in oneself, it may be time for some self-reflection, and creation of an approach and plan to address the issues, to be a better boss.

Middleton D. Five Signs You're a Bad Boss. Wall Street Journal, February 14, 2011.

to delegate *etc.*, the report needs to try to discuss in as diplomatic manner as possible, and not have significant expectations in the short term – change can be difficult, resistance may be great (even if evidence is present), and patience is a virtue. Recall that an assessment on the perspective that the supervisor may be taking (the organizational lens) may not be the same as yours. At the end of the day, the motivation is that you want to do your job better to ensure a benefit to the organization (and your supervisor, whom you have identified their goals and objectives in their specific *milieu*). Making this clear is the best one can do in order to try to address the situation. Unless the transgressions are so great they have legal or quasi-legal ramifications, the approaches need to be rational and stepwise. When to decide that either the situation cannot be fixed and/or others need to be involved (human resources, recruiters to other organizations, *i.e.* changing jobs, *etc.*) is so individual that general rules cannot apply, except that communication is the initial step.

REFERENCES

Bolman, L.G., Deal, T.E., 2008. Reframing Organizations: Artistry, Choice and Leadership, fourth ed. Jossey-Bass, San Francisco.

Drucker, P.F., 2006. The Effective Executive: The Definitive Guide to Getting the Right Things Done (Revised). HarperCollins, New York.

Kroeger, O., Thuesen, J.M., Rutledge, H., 2002. Type talk at Work (revised): How the 16 Personality Types Determine Your Success on the Job. Delta, New York.

Sutton, R.I., 2010. Good Boss, Bad Boss: How to Be the Best…and Learn from the Worst. Business Plus, New York.

Being the CEO (or At Least Acting Like One)

"The best CEOs I know are teachers, and at the core of what they teach is strategy".

-Michael Porter

"The reason that the dot-com companies didn't succeed is that they were very good at the science end but they didn't understand anything about the art of buying and selling merchandise. They thought that was the easy part but it turned out to be the most difficult".

-James Sinegal

"Great CEOs are not just born with shiny hair and a tie. "

-Marc Andreessen

KNOW THYSELF

Taking on broad corporate responsibility is a personal choice. Particularly for the technical executive, the additional skills that need be exercised on a daily basis may draw one far afield from the rigors of scientific investigation and product development. Nonetheless, there are excellent examples of those who have made the transition successfully, in a variety of different industries, and with a variety of different backgrounds, from academic basic researcher, industrial scientist, chemical engineer, and physician scientist – the list is extensive. Certainly, an advantage of most technical individuals, as noted throughout this book, is the analytical abilities required for most scientific and engineering endeavors, which can be translated into analysis of other areas for both issue

Managing and Leading for Science Professionals. http://dx.doi.org/10.1016/B978-0-12-416686-8.00014-1

identification and problem solving, as long as this, in turn, can be converted into action, oftentimes with less data than one would like. As has been discussed, with increases in managerial and leadership responsibility, the level of data generation responsibility declines, and decisions based on risk and uncertainty increase, which is a fundamental aspect of any CEO's job. Waiting for more data, notwithstanding generating it, many times is not possible if the organization is to maintain competitive advantage in a given set of circumstances; and as well, needing to understand other areas of the financial and commercial parts of the firm, and exercising judgment therein, is yet another managerial muscle to be exercised with higher levels of corporate responsibility. All of this is underpinned by working through others, understanding their needs, and creating a motivating environment with a compelling vision for the future. Making the transition to this corporate *milieu* involves knowing oneself, and what is fulfilling on a personal and professional level, including the realization that this decision will challenge in different ways, most of which are outside of the classic technical realm.

Indeed, an area that is quite challenging to become accustomed to, and where many have seen significant difficulty with technical personnel as they move up into the corporate ladder, is that often there is no "right answer", and that the interpretation of what is considered data has many different degrees of freedom. It is important for those wishing to adopt a more corporate role to be able to deal with this type of ambiguity, given the disparate sources of information (which may be less than robust given the standards acceptable to technical personnel) needing to be interpreted. This is not so much a failing as an issue of familiarity; however, a lack of tolerance to this type of situation may suggest that these types of roles may not be suitable for those who have a technical background. Only by self-assessment and reflection, often with the help of mentors and colleagues, can one determine whether this type of role is desired or appropriate. Having a firm understanding of career goals, and the types of responsibilities inherent within general managerial roles, is paramount, as the transition from the technical to the corporate is not necessarily for the faint of heart; most time is spent on non-scientific rather than technical ones. One technical CEO once noted to me that when he was a scientific VP, there were always two lines outside his office; one very long one, with staff most often asking him to troubleshoot or deal with a specific (mostly technical) issue, and a very short one, where people were reporting good news/data; when he became the CEO, there still were two lines – the long one was where people had problems and especially complaints, and the short one ("very short") were those who didn't (but still had specific issues nonetheless). Certainly, this is not an infrequent occurrence, but going into the situation with full understanding and willingness to face those challenges can be a most fulfilling experience.

"Know yourself. Don't accept your dog's admiration as conclusive evidence that you are wonderful".

-Eppie Lederer

SETTING DIRECTION AND DRIVING THE BUS

There is a paradox within leadership and management especially apparent in the CEO suite, in that while needing to set the strategy and objectives, the higher in the hierarchy one rises to, the less one knows about the specifics. As much as some would desire to still be able to do the latest experiments in the lab to determine whether a new mechanism of action is correct, or to put a personal touch on the pivotal clinical trial that will be used to test a late stage compound, executive responsibilities around motivation and direction often drive our actions toward other areas, appropriately so. By being self-aware, and knowing our responsibilities need reflect the part of the organization that we are in, clearly there are opportunity costs for which to be accounted; the jobs of the executives are to ensure that the resources are provided to the staff to be able to perform their jobs; we as leaders are enablers and facilitators. This relates to being able to work through others, recognizing their strengths and areas of development, as well as their career anchors and professional aspirations. At the CEO level, the job is similar, except the diversity of staff is higher, the needs are more intense, and the attention paid to the company human resources is significant (see below). The mandate is also more broad, in that the responsibility encompasses setting a direction (with whatever board or overseeing body is used) by understanding the external environment with objectives formulated for value (however defined) creation. That leadership function needs to be able to be combined with the managerial one, ensuring resources and support are sufficient for the functional areas to carry out their respective roles, whether that is R&D, finance, marketing/sales, manufacturing and operations, or IT. Of note is that we as technical managers be wary that we allocate more resources preferentially to those functions with which we are most familiar; this is a common occurrence, albeit unconscious, due to our most likely more detailed knowledge of the area. Hence, both strategically and operationally, once accepting a more corporate role, we must be able to articulate the vision and execute – both map out the destination and drive the bus. While larger organizations may split these responsibilities to some extent, fundamentally both areas need be considered when in a corporate role.

"Strategy without tactics is the slowest route to victory. Tactics without strategy is the noise before defeat".

-Sun Tzu

Despite having a broader role, and by definition not having the same sophistication in the scientific and technical realm that one had earlier in one's career, learning continues to be a key aspect within one's corporate responsibility. As noted in the chapter on mentorship, the acquisition of new knowledge, as well as its dissemination through mentor/mentee relations with others, is an important area not to ignore; being a better leader, manager, and/or scientist or engineer, and improving skills in finance, sales, marketing, and corporate strategy is always on the curriculum of the corporate manager in order to both understand the external and internal parts of the organizational *milieu* within which one works. Certainly, this responsibility to be curious allows the ability to ask pertinent questions that might clarify or at least inform on what issues need to be considered at the highest levels, as well as continue to develop the firm in the direction which is both motivating and value creating. While we may not be able to design the final prototype of the next product in a given franchise, we can certainly create the strategy by which its attributes can best be communicated to the customer and stakeholders.

COMMUNICATION...AGAIN

It goes without saying that communication is an important aspect in the corporate suites. Communication with reports, as well as both internal and external audiences, is an important aspect of the corporate role. While all of the concepts regarding communication mentioned in earlier chapters apply, there is an additional difference when representing the company *per se* to these diverse audiences. The content that is communicated from corporate view may have a material effect on how the company is perceived, given the position of the person who is doing the communicating. It is important to invest the time and effort to be proficient in all types of these communications – the ability to maintain such consistency is of key importance in the leadership role. Further, especially if a corporate officer, statements made both internally at public forums as well as to outside audiences represent the organization, and hence have potential effects on actions by others, such as investors, collaborators, and those involved in the extended enterprise. In the public company realm, there are clear ramifications on these aspects, often highly regulated (*e.g.* by the Security and Exchange Commission in the U.S.), but even in the private firm world, these can affect how both customers and suppliers view the organization. Hence, as a manager, it is always important what is said as well as how it is said, but as a corporate officer, it reflects what the company represents as well. Thus, communication remains a relevant aspect when the technical executive moves toward a corporate role, not only as the management of staff within the division, but also toward external audiences and stakeholders. While this may seem common sense, I have heard commentary from senior C-level individuals to institutional investors as a joke about product margins, which was then reprinted by several news organizations. Thoughtful preparation prior to statements to internal and external audiences is perhaps the better part of valor.

"Wit without discretion is a sword in the hand of a fool".

-Spanish Proverb

Another aspect about communication in general about the organization revolves around the messages that have been derived from the corporate team. While as technical executives we often have "FAQs" (frequently asked questions) about some product releases and/or the pipeline within the firm, it is incumbent upon corporate executives to also be clear about the other, more commercial aspects of the firm. Again, this relates to the corporate executive to be a representation of the company, vis-à-vis the various activities that are ongoing and myriad within any organization, from finance to manufacturing. Certainly, as noted earlier, this takes a learning of a new vocabulary and/or potentially refreshing the knowledge around microeconomics and product life cycle that were learned as more junior executives, but I have found it pays dividends particularly when dealing with financial professionals outside of the organizational world.

EVEN MORE SO, IT'S ABOUT THE PEOPLE

My experience within different organizations large and small is that as one moves up the hierarchy, one definitely appreciates the jobs that all of the staff perform on a daily basis in order to make an organization run and create value for shareholders. Indeed, a well-performing company is so apparent from all viewpoints – internal, external, stakeholders, and casual observers, since one sees employees who are productive, motivated, and excited about what they do – one can hear it in the voices of the employees who work with customers as well as those who work "backroom". Obviously, our job as technical executives is to generate this motivation along with the direction derived from the corporate strategy; as a corporate executive, it is also to maintain the motivation of the entire team, as well as help craft the strategy of the firm. Within this is what most executives I have spoken with take as a key responsibility within the motivational aspect: talent management. One of the largest responsibilities we have is to both hire and retain the best talent for the job for the benefit of the firm; it is no mean feat, and takes a considerable amount of experience to be sure that the right person is in the right job, and can be motivated (and motivate others) toward the mission of the firm. In the past, this was often delegated to a human resources function, but today, this is much more a partnership between the hiring manager(s) and the HR function; it is too important not to have each functional area deeply involved. Corporate executives, and especially the CEOs, must act to both encourage and create the infrastructure where the best and the brightest can be found, retained, and advanced (if desired – see Chapter 2, gatekeeper function). Without good people, no organization can survive and prosper, and seeing this from a perspective of a myriad of groups coming together to produce an excellent product or service is both astounding, and creates an appreciation of those who do their job well. And not unexpectedly, providing the team visible expressions of appreciation and gratitude is an important function to motivate and create the environment and culture where the best and the brightest want to come to work.

"The conventional definition of management is getting work done through people, but real management is developing people through work."

-Agha Hasan Abedi

Feeling Appreciated: Jack Welch at GE

Jack Welch (now retired) was the former Chairman and CEO of GE. During his time at the helm, he created more growth than any other CEO ever – from a market capitalization of $12B in 1981 to $475B when he retired in 2000. This was more than what Bill Gates, Andy Grove, or Warren Buffet are delivering or have delivered during their times as CEOs. Welch has always emphasized both talent management and teaching at the GE "Crotonville" Campus, where managers hear directly from the boss around strategy, priorities, human resources, and/or services. His conversion of the company from a stolid, formal culture to one of informality and innovation was profound. Ironically, this could have been a quite different history if not for a Reuben Gutoff. Back in 1960, Jack Welch was hired as a junior engineer by GE in the plastics division of the Pittsfield, MA office. However, in less than a year, he had decided to quit, and had accepted another job in Skokie, IL, working for International Minerals & Chemicals; he felt unappreciated, as well as suppressed by the bureaucracy of the company. He once noted that the minimal raise he had been given was "offensive", and decided it was time to leave. Reuben Gutoff, a junior technical executive who was above Welch, recognized his talent and wanted to keep him with the company. Despite the fact that his farewell party was two days away, he persuaded Welch and his wife to go out to dinner with him in order to convince him to stay. Gutoff promised Welch that he would create a small company environment for him, and would help him avoid the GE red tape that was so problematic for the young engineer. With Gutoff's prodding, Welch decided that he would stay at GE – and would still have the party, "because I like parties". The small company within a big company has been a key theme within his management style at GE, as well as believing in and expressing of appreciation for the people at the firm. It is both sobering and encouraging to think that the future of GE was saved by a junior executive who recognized the talent of a junior engineer, and was willing to show appreciation for that individual. Who might be the next Jack Welch within our midst?

Welch J, Byrne JA. *Jack Welch: Straight from the Gut*. New York, Business Plus, 2003.

DEEP DIVES

One key element that I learned from a mentor was that occasionally, in problems or projects that have "crossed the yellow line" (a reference to car manufacturing, when on the assembly line a worker physically crosses the line to do his job something has gone wrong), a detailed root cause analysis is required – and needs to be performed by senior managers, often referring to corporate management, including the CEO. While our jobs are typically at a high level in most instances, occasionally when we see a problem that recurs, or when there is a material impact on the organization, we need to step in and look more carefully at the situation. While this may seem somewhat contradictory given the discussion on the need to delegate and the reduction in expertise as one moves up the ladder, in fact, our experiences in being able to analyze situations, whether they be corporate or scientific, can be of assistance to ask the right questions to the people on the ground who know most about the process or product with which there is a key issue. This is not to overrule or overstep the managers and staff working on the issue; in fact, this should be completed with all involved in order to best assess the situation. While this is not done in every circumstance, it has been seen to be of value in a variety of different settings, from manufacturing of cars (Toyota Production System) to that of CT scanners (GE Medical Systems). Indeed, Jack Welch, the former Chairman and CEO of GE, was well known to do deep dives and fly to plants across the country unannounced in order to assess a situation first hand. Despite the schedules of busy corporate executives, this is an important component that we need not forget in discharging our responsibilities – rolling up the proverbial sleeves is occasionally required. But as noted previously, our role is to help decipher the problem, and help the team closest to the issue figure out an approach; we do not have all the answers, and are facilitators toward the solution.

A derivative about deep dives that relates to motivation is the willingness always to be part of the team. While position creates responsibilities, despite being in the corporate suite, we must be willing to work on teams in any situation, whether it is packing boxes as noted (Chapter 4; Gordon Binder) to making buffers in the lab, it is important that we are willing to do what is needed for the best performance of the team. While I am sure that the scientists at the companies with whom I worked would much prefer that I not do the PCR for an experiment, and rather participate in an earnings call or board presentation, nonetheless whether it is to act as example during a volunteer event that the company sponsors or give awards at the company meetings, our participation on the team as a visible members can be motivating for the team and quite fulfilling for us.

TIME IS NOT YOUR OWN

One area that many corporate executives and CEOs have mentioned to me is that when adopting this role, there was a significant loss of control of their schedules. It has been previously mentioned that time is the most precious resource that one has, as moving up the ranks of the organization necessarily requires more time to be spent with others (see also above). The need to prioritize becomes especially relevant in this regard, and being able to say *no* to other commitments outside of those within the realm of responsibility becomes an important skill. One needs to be realistic with oneself in order to meet the changing time commitments, since oftentimes our lack of control of our *milieu* does not allow us to commit to other activities. This is a balancing act, since at the same time being available for people in the company, helping out in any way possible, mentoring, and being mentored are all important aspects of the day-to-day responsibilities of the corporate team members. Hence, being very cognizant of what is on and not on your schedule is very important, as the time

A Deep Dive: Steve Jobs and the iPod

Jack Welch was a believer in the deep dive, where he noted, "It's spotting a challenge where you think you can make a difference...then throwing the weight of your position behind it". Indeed, sometimes doing a deep dive encompasses driving projects to a given endpoint, which can be as far as the marketplace. Steve Jobs was well known for pushing the agenda on certain projects that he felt had particular strategic value to the company, which could be considered a deep dive in accordance with Welch's quote. His interest in music and music devices was one such area, where he personally pushed the schedule for development and release. In the case of the development of the iPod, Jobs effected a paradigm shift in design for the company; by placing significant pressure on the timelines for development, he forced Apple away from the old system of unique chips, disc drives, and operating systems to one where integration of outsourced materials with the Apple components was the only way to meet anticipated launch dates. Further, Jobs participated in the target product profile of the different iPods, and negotiated personally with record labels to both get their music into iTunes as well as ensure the (then) consistent $.99 per song price. The development of the iPod created a juggernaut in the electronic entertainment business, highly defined by Jobs, from the niche computer company that it had been before.

Welch J, Byrne JA. Jack Welch: Straight from the Gut. New York, Business Plus, 2003.

Young JS, Simon WL. iCon: Steve Jobs, the greatest second act in the history of business. Hoboken, Wiley, 2005.

on the calendar becomes much more controlled by others than by you. I know that it is something that I was initially unprepared for, but only with a very disciplined and helpful assistant was I able to make time for all that was required of me. Indeed, an invaluable piece of advice given to me by a former CEO was that specifically allocating time to administrative support, "enabling your administrative support to enable you", is paramount, where clear direction on prioritization of life areas from family to health maintenance and vacations and downtime are defined. Being a bottleneck due to a backed up schedule does not help you, your organization, or those who depend on you.

Moreover, prepare your family with respect to time commitments once accepting a corporate set of responsibilities. Oftentimes there is just not enough time during the day to accomplish all that you need – it requires some additional time that once was considered "off hours". Unfortunately, there are (many) times when those responsibilities are extended – one executive compared it to like a warm pie, as it eventually spreads to encompass everything on your plate. There are dinners to attend and/or host, talks at conferences to give, and late meetings to discuss emergent issues, or calls at strange hours to accommodate partners in different time zones, *etc*. Again, in the global economy, travel and these types of activities might be considered for some *de rigeur*, but for those who have labored in the laboratory, and only occasionally needed to take a trip to a conference to give a talk, this can be quite eye-opening (fortunately, technology such as webinars can alleviate some of these types of pressures). This is not to say these are impossible issues, only that they need to be managed, as one manages an ever bursting-at-the-seams schedule. As stated once by an anonymous senior manager, "Optimization by organization, prioritization and deputization!"

"Yesterday is a canceled check. Tomorrow is a promissory note. Today is the only cash you have so spend it wisely".

-Kay Lyons

THE BOARD

The Board, whether it is a Board of Directors (typically for for-profit firms) or Board of Trustees (for non- or not-for-profit organizations), is involved with oversight as well as guidance on strategic objectives and goals. Depending on the type of firm, the Board may be as little as a handful of persons such as in private companies, or up to 20 or more, as trustees of a specific charitable organization. As well, the makeup of these groups can be markedly different; early stage companies that are venture backed may have investors (*e.g.* venture capitalists) on the board, while established public companies may have a more diverse set of directors, from inside and outside the industry. It is tacitly assumed these individuals should have experiences that can help in setting strategy of the organization in question, based on similar domain or other appropriate skills. As such, the Board should be supportive in the guidance around strategic initiatives to care for the interests of all stakeholders. The management team is responsible for participation in the formulation of the strategy of the organization, based on detailed knowledge of the business (broadly defined) and as well, has the responsibility to execute on the strategic plan.

For the technical and/or corporate executive, this may be the first time one is exposed to this type of management, and indeed, has been identified in surveys of new CEOs as a particular area where familiarity was scant. Indeed, the dynamic can be quite different from a reporting structure, since the Board (typically with the exception of the CEO) consists of individuals who are not employees, but by definition are outside the organization. A key responsibility of the corporate management (and especially the CEO) is to interface with these board members to best ensure the strategy of the company is either moving forward or identify challenges on whether a course correction is needed. Further, another aspect to be cognizant is that the level of detail of company operations may not be either apparent or understood by directors, and thus, may require regular updates to ensure an appreciation of the consistency of the tactics of the company with the strategy; this is particularly true if there is less domain experience on the Board. As opposed to organizational employees, where interactions are fairly frequent, the non-employee status of the directors can be quite challenging for a new CEO or corporate executive to manage, as the interactions are much less frequent than that of members of the management team. It is wise to be cognizant of this, and prepare accordingly with respect to communication plans and opportunities to interact.

Because good boards will have experienced individuals as directors, often leaders of their own organizations, there may at times be some level of conflict on a particular strategic direction. With several CEOs in a room with different experiences, it is not surprising that differences of opinion can crop up when discussing strategy to move forward. The corporate executive may need to be prepared to be a go-between, advocate, consensus builder, and/or cajoler in coming up with a reasonable strategy that is significantly robust to drive the organization forward in a way that the respective execution of strategy and tactics from the management level may be performed. As in any case of managing upward, it is clear that the alignment of goals is an important aspect in this exercise; it is also important to understand that the Board or a specific director's goals may *not* align with that of the company, due to specific timeframes for generation of liquidity, outside pressures on specific board members, different perceptions of stakeholder interests *etc.* One needs to be prepared for these situations, being aware of the potential that they may arise, with an approach of unquestioned legitimacy, using cogent arguments and/or mechanisms to address such issues and come to an agreement of the best thing to do for the organization as a whole. These can be quite challenging situations, and mentorship from those who have faced this situation can be invaluable. As well, oftentimes utilizing outside resources (especially seasoned executives from other organizations) can be quite helpful in providing data that can frame strategic decisions in a more clarifying way; indeed, having two or three individuals well-versed in the industry, not associated with the company, but who can provide advice to you is an invaluable "kitchen cabinet". The corporate executive/CEO needs to understand that these are options that could be considered when dealing with such circumstances with the Board or a specific director.

REFERENCES

Bossidy, L., Charan, R., 2002. Execution: The Discipline of Getting Things Done. Crown Business, New York.

Conaty, B., Charan, R., 2010. The Talent Masters: Why Smart Leaders Put People Before Numbers. Crown Business, New York.

Jennings, K., Stahl-Wert, J., 2004. The Serving Leader. Berrett-Koehler, San Francisco.

Johnson, C.R., 1998. CEO Logic: How to Think and Act Like a Chief Executive. Career Press, Pompton Plains.

A Final Note

I have always been excited about being able to see data of experiments that had been performed, whether it was to determine whether we had pulled out a new interesting gene sequence, or to find out the results of a clinical trial where we had hoped that a new treatment for cancer was effective; for me, the joy of discovery is simply one of the most gratifying professional aspects I've ever experienced. Moving from that to other types of professional satisfaction, such as seeing the accomplishments of others, while not for everyone, can also be significantly and equally fulfilling. Presumably, because you are reading this book, you are considering that transition as well. In the preceding chapters, there has been a discussion on a variety of topics, with one specific theme: *What I'd wished I'd known* as I entered into and moved up the management ladder. The book focuses on *you*, the technical executive or executive-to-be, in some of the new challenges that you may face as your role changes. I have tried to collect both personal experiences as well as the experiences of others who have managed the transition to technical executive (and beyond), and provide both the lessons learned (and re-learned) encountered along the way. The hope is that this at least provides the framework by which your transition and evolution can be more easily facilitated, particularly as the levels of responsibilities increase. While this book has concentrated on you, many other books, articles, and media are more general, with a more broad orientation. I've listed some of these below, which could be helpful as you move through your journey as technical executive and manager. My hope is that this text will help you along the way traversing these brave new worlds, and may I sincerely wish you the best of luck in what I hope to be a fruitful and beneficial voyage.

MANAGEMENT

Freeman, R.E., 2010. Strategic Management: A Stakeholder Approach. Cambridge University Press, Cambridge.

McAfee, A., 2012. Enterprise 2.0: New Collaborative Tools for Your Organization's Toughest Challenges. Harvard Business Press, Cambridge.

Managing and Leading for Science Professionals. http://dx.doi.org/10.1016/B978-0-12-416686-8.00015-3
149

Reason, J., 2000. Human Error: Models and Management. British Medical Journal 320, 768–770.

Szulanski, G., 2000. The Process of Knowledge Transfer: A Diachronic Analysis of Stickiness. Organizational Behavior and Human Decision Processes 82, 9–27.

LEADERSHIP

Goleman, D., 2000. Working with Emotional Intelligence. Bantam, New York.

Harvard Business Review's 10 Must Reads On Leadership. Harvard Business Review Press, Cambridge, 2011.

Judge, T.A., Bono, J.E., Ilies, R., Gerhardt, M.W., 2002. Personality and Leadership: A Qualitative and Quantitative Review. Journal of Applied Psychology 87, 765–780.

Kaye, B., Jordan-Evans, S., 2008. Love'em or Lose'em: Getting Good People to Stay. Berett-Koehler, San Francisco.

Mintzberg, H., 1998. Covert Leadership: notes on managing professionals. Knowledge Workers respond to inspiration, not supervision. Harvard Business Review Nov-Dec 76, 140–147.

ENTREPRENEURSHIP

Drucker, P.F., 2006. Innovation and Entrepreneurship. HarperBusiness, New York.

Ries, E., 2011. The Lean Startup: How Today's Entrepreneurs Use Continuous Innovation to Create Radically Successful Businesses. Crown Business, New York.

Sexton, D.L., Bowman, N., 1985. The Entrepreneur: A Capable Executive and More. Journal of Business Venturing 1, 129–140.

Shah, S.K., Tripsas, M., 2007. The Accidental Entrepreneur: The Emergent and Collective Process of User Entrepreneurship. Strategic Entrepreneurship Journal 1, 123–140.

Shooter, S.B., Evans, C.M., Simpson, T.W., 2007. Building a Better Ice Scraper – A Case in Product Platforms for the Entrepreneur. Journal of Intelligent Manufacturing 18, 159–170.

STRATEGY

Arora, A., Fosfuri, A., Gambardella, A., 2004. Markets for Technology: The Economics of Innovation and Corporate Strategy. MIT Press, Cambridge.

Collis, D., Montgomery, C., 2004. Corporate Strategy, second ed. McGraw-Hill/Irwin, New York.

Hamel, G., Prahalad, C.K., 1996. Competing for the Future. Harvard Business Review Press, Cambridge.

Harvard Business Review's 10 Must Reads on Strategy. Harvard Business Review Press, Cambridge, 2011.

INNOVATION

Adams, R., Bessant, J., Phelps, R., 2006. Innovation Management Measurement: A Review. International Journal of Management Reviews 8, 21–47.

Berkun, S., 2010. The Myths of Innovation. O'Reilly, Cambridge.

Christensen, C.M., Raynor, M.E., 2003. The Innovator's Solution: Creating and Sustaining Successful Growth. Harvard Business School Press, Cambridge.

Desouza, K.C., 2011. Intrapreneurship: Managing Ideas Within Your Organization. University of Toronto Press, Toronto.

Utterback, J.M., 1996. Mastering the Dynamics of Innovation. Harvard Business Review Press, Cambridge.

CHANGE MANAGEMENT

Bishop, E.B., 2011. Identities as Lenses. Administrative Science Quarterly 56, 61–94.

Keyton, J., 2010. Communication & Organizational Culture: A Key to Understanding Work Experiences. Sage, Thousand Oaks.

Kotter, J.P., 2012. Leading Change. Harvard Business Review Press, Cambridge.

Sirkin, H.L., Keenan, P., Jackson, A., 2005. The Hard Side of Change Management. Harvard Business Review 83, 108–118.

Todnem, R., 2005. Organisational Change Management: A Critical Review. Journal of Change Management 5, 369–380.

PODCASTS (ALL AVAILABLE ON iTUNES)

The Economist Podcast
The EntreLeadership Podcast
Entrepreneurial Thought Leaders Podcast
Harvard Business IdeaCast Podcast
Leadership Podcasts from LeaderNetwork.org
London School of Economics Podcast
Manager Tools Podcasts

GENERAL WEBSITES

Entrepreneur Magazine http://www.entrepreneur.com/magazine/index.html
Harvard Business Review http://hbr.org
Human Resources About.com http://humanresources.about.com
INSEAD http://knowledge.insead.edu
London School of Economics and Political Science http://www2.lse.ac.uk/home.aspx
MIT Sloan Management Review http://sloanreview.mit.edu
Strategy+Business http:// www.strategy-business.com

Index

Note: Page numbers followed by "f" denote figures; "t" tables.

A

Absorptive capacity
    inherent knowledge base 127
    role in 126–127
    underdeveloped nations 127b–128b
Active listening
    downsteam effects 46–47
    interpersonal interaction 48
    techniques 47–48, 47t
Adopter segments 61–62, 62t
Ambidextrous approach 64–65
Autonomy/independence 23t, 25
    diverse organizations 26
    needs and motivations 25–26

B

Balance sheet 50–51
Balanced approach 101
Bearing risk 60
Bilateral rate 51. *See also* Spot rate.
Board, the 147
    experiencing individuals as directors 148
    for technical and/or corporate
        executive 147–148
Boundary impedance 107–108
Breakout innovation 60–61
Brian's group 120–121
Business decisions 59
Business project 120
    Brian's group 120–121
    paralysis by analysis 122
    R&D 120
    relative degrees of freedom *v*. corporate
        alignment 121f
    respective hypotheses 120
    technical executive role 121

C

CAD. *See* Computer-aided design
CAM. *See* Computer-aided manufacturing
Career anchor 22–23
    autonomy/independence 25
        diverse organizations 26

needs and motivations 25–26
    categories 23
    internal and external career 22–23
    lifestyle 30–31
        archetype 31–32
        quality of life choice 31
    managerial competence
        cross-functional coordination 25
        managerial role 24–25
    security 27
    sense of service 28–29
        chronic problems 29
        modus operandi 29
    skunk works 30
    stability 27
    summary of 23t
    technical competence
        gatekeepers 23–24
        technical executives 24
    "technical executive" 22
Cautionary note 68
CEO
    Board, the 147
        individuals as directors 148
        for technical and/or corporate
            executive 147–148
    communication 142
        commercial aspects of firm
            142–143
    corporate responsibility 139–140
    data generation responsibility 139–140
    data interpretation 140
    deep dives 144–145
        Jack Welch about 144–145
        Steve Jobs and iPod 146b
        willingness 145
    driving bus 141
    concerning employees 143
    importance of learning 141–142
    Jack Welch 144b
    setting direction 141
    time management 145–147
Certainty 60, 69
Clockspeed 126b
Coaches 111

Printed and bound by CPI Group (UK) Ltd, Croydon, CR0 4YY

08/05/2025

01864886-0002